THE SCOTTISH TARTANS

WITH HISTORICAL SKETCHES OF THE CLANS AND FAMILIES OF SCOTLAND

REVISED BY SIR THOMAS INNES OF LEARNEY
LORD LYON KING OF ARMS

THE ARMS OF CHIEFS OF CLANS AND FAMILIES AND CLANSMEN'S BADGES

ILLUSTRATED BY WILLIAM SEMPLE

W. & A. K. JOHNSTON & G. W. BACON LTD.
EDINA WORKS, EASTER ROAD, EDINBURGH, SCOTLAND
30 MUSEUM STREET, LONDON, W.C.1

Second Revised Edition	.	. .	1945
Reprinted	. . .	. .	1946
Reprinted	. . .	. .	1949
Reprinted	. . .	. .	1951
Reprinted	. . .	. .	1953
Reprinted	. . .	. .	1955
Reprinted	. . .	. .	1957
Revised and Enlarged Edition	.		1961

Printed in Great Britain by W. & A. K. Johnston & G. W. Bacon Ltd.

THE SCOTTISH TARTANS
INTRODUCTION

IN this book you will find the following information:

101 Scottish Tartans in colour;

91 Arms of Clan Chiefs;

81 Clansmen's Badges;

36 Plant Badges of the Clans;

Alphabetical List of surnames indicating the Clan with which each family is connected.

TARTANS

Tartan describes the distinctive chequered pattern generally worked out in a woven material such as woollen cloth. Formerly the colours came from vegetable dyes concocted by infusing various local roots, mosses and flowers. Now, of course, chemical dyes are used, but these can be skilfully modified to impart a soft, mellow hue which gives the new length of tartan an " ancient " appearance. Though such tartan material is a characteristically Scottish product, weavers and dyers in other countries have also produced attractive chequered designs which are entitled to be called tartans. The ones shown in this book, however, are those of various Scottish clans. You will notice as you look through the pages that a great range of designs is possible. Each particular pattern is known as a " sett " and a length of tartan repeats this design as often as required.

Everyone is familiar with the kilt worn by Scottish regiments and pipe-bands and by many Scotsmen. The ancient dress of the Scottish Highlander, however, was not a kilt of this type, but a belted plaid. This plaid (the *féileadh-mór* or " great wrap ") was a generous length of tartan cloth about 16–18 feet long and 6 feet wide. The upper portion covered the wearer's shoulders. It was belted at the waist and the lower portion hung down to the knees. By the early part of the eighteenth century the lower half of the belted plaid (the *féileadh-beag* or "little wrap") was in general use as a kilt. And since then the kilt has been the traditional garb of the Highlander as regimental uniform, at Highland Games and outdoor activities, on social occasions such as weddings and dances, and to-day, of course, many Highlanders use it as everyday wear.

The great dividing-line in the history of Scottish tartans was the Jacobite Rising of 1745. After the defeat of Prince Charles Edward Stuart and his Highland followers, various Acts of Parliament were passed, the aim of which was to disarm the Highlanders and to destroy the clan spirit by prohibiting the wearing of traditional Highland dress. This ban lasted for thirty-six years and one of its unhappy consequences was that the age-old methods of using vegetable dyes were not passed on to the next generation.

In the late eighteenth and early nineteenth centuries there was a considerable literary resurgence of Scottish national feeling. Robert Burns, for example, wrote " Scots Wha Hae " and Lady Nairne wrote the haunting Jacobite refrain " Will Ye No' Come Back Again ? " Even more important was the influence of Sir Walter Scott. The publication of such poems as " The Lady of the Lake " and such novels as " Waverley " and " Rob Roy " did much to awaken a widespread interest in Scottish scenery and to arouse an admiration for the Highlander as a picturesque and romantic figure. And the literary movement had its counterpart in Sir Henry Raeburn's magnificent tartan-clad Chiefs. When King George IV made his first excursion north of the Border, Scott stage-managed the ceremonies and there was a tremendous rash of tartan in Edinburgh. Queen Victoria was proud of her Stuart ancestors and Balmoral burgeoned in tartan furnishings and kilted gillies.

At the present day there is no doubt about the lasting popularity of tartan. True, one can have too much in the way of mass-produced tartan-decorated souvenirs, but as a dress material tartan has an enduring appeal. Certainly few women visitors can resist the temptation of a well-cut tartan skirt worn with fine Scottish woollens. And for day or evening wear the kilt—a masterpiece of skilled tailoring—shows the clansman at his most virile and elegant.

CLANS

The basis of the clan is a family—a principal family together with its offshoots and branches.

In Scotland, clan came to mean a group of families occupying a definite locality—a particular glen, for example, or an island. These families shared—or claimed to share—their descent from a common ancestor. The head of the group was the living " Representer " of this ancestor and as such he was chief of the clan. To him the clansmen owed loyalty and respect. They accepted his jurisdiction over their daily affairs and responded to his summons in time of battle. The chief, in turn, was the patriarch—the head and leader of the clan. In return for their personal devotion to him, he had an obligation to protect his followers and to give help to any of them who were in distress.

By the reign of King James VI the localities occupied by the various clans were fairly well-defined—though liable of course to be increased or diminished as circumstances altered. In each of these clan districts the local weavers produced a distinctive local tartan pattern or " sett." Thus members of the same clan probably wore the particular tartan woven and dyed in their own neighbourhood. It would be misleading, however, to raise this practical convenience to a rule and say that in the seventeenth century each clan had its own special tartan and wore it as a sort of " uniform." The distinctive sett adopted by the chief and his relatives became traditionally the " Clan Tartan " and when the statutory ban on Highland dress was removed in 1782 the wearing of clan tartan was a matter of pride. The tartans shown in this book are " authentic "—that is to say, the sett has been defined by the chief of the clan (from family portraits and other evidence) to the satisfaction of the Lyon Court and the description is officially recorded in the *Public Register of All Arms and Bearings*.

PLANT BADGES

The plant badge of a clansman was a sprig fixed on a staff, spear or bonnet. Obviously incapable of being a distinguishing emblem or mark, there is ground for believing that it was the clan's charm-plant, like an amulet or talisman. On page 16 you will find a list of the plant badges of the different clans and on page 17 are shown thirty-six examples in colour.

CHIEF'S ARMS

From page 18 onwards you will find plates showing clan tartans in colour and at the top right-hand side you will see the personal arms of the chief of the clan. These arms consist of the SHIELD on which various heraldic charges are displayed, a HELMET, varying in design to indicate the wearer's rank, and MANTLING (a covering to protect the helmet from the sun). At the top is the CREST resting on a WREATH. At either side of the shield are the SUPPORTERS, indicating in this case that the arms are those of a great chief. There is also a MOTTO (or possibly two) enscrolled above the crest or below the shield. These arms are the personal property of the holder and it is an offence for anyone else to misappropriate them.

CLANSMEN'S BADGES

On most pages you will see a clansman's badge in the lower left-hand corner. The chief himself wears a crested badge surmounted by three feathers. It was the practice, however, for chiefs to allow their followers to wear the crest and motto in a silver strap-and-buckle badge. This is the clansman's badge and if you are a member of the clan you may wear it. If a clan lacks a chief, no clansman's badge is shown.

ALPHABETICAL LIST OF
FAMILY NAMES

Pages 7–15 contain an alphabetical list of family names. Many people are entitled to wear a particular tartan or clansman's badge who are not aware of it. This list will help you to trace the connection, if any, between your family name and the clan to which you may be connected. If you are a member of a clan sept, you can wear the sept tartan if one is available—otherwise choose the tartan of the clan with which you are connected.

ALPHABETICAL LIST OF FAMILY NAMES

Showing the Clan connection

Family Name.	Connected with Clan.
Abbot	Macnab.
Abbotson	Do.
Abernethy	Leslie.
Adam	Gordon.
Adamson	Mackintosh.
Adie	Gordon.
Airlie	Ogilvie.
Alexander	MacAlister, MacDonell of Glengarry.
Allan	MacDonald of Clanranald, MacFarlane.
Allanson	Do. do.
Allardice	Graham of Menteith.
Alpin	MacAlpine.
Anderson	Ross.
Andrew	Do.
Angus	Macinnes.
Armstrong	Armstrong.
Arthur	MacArthur (Campbell of Strachur).
Ayson	Mackintosh (Shaw).
Bain	Mackay.
Baird	Baird.
Bannatyne	Campbell of Argyll, Stuart of Bute.
Bannerman	Forbes.
Barclay	Barclay.
Bard	Baird.
Bartholomew	MacFarlane.
Baxter	Macmillan.
Bayne	Mackay.
Bean	MacBean.
Beath	MacDonald, Maclean of Duart.
Beaton	MacDonald, Maclean of Duart, MacLeod of Harris.
Bell	Macmillan.
Berkeley	Barclay.
Bethune, Beton	MacDonald, MacLeod of Harris.
Black	Lamont, MacGregor, Maclean of Duart.
Bontein	Graham of Menteith.
Bouchannane	Buchanan.
Bowie	MacDonald.
Boyd	Stewart (Royal).
Brebner, Bremner	Farquharson.
Brieve	Morrison.
Brodie	Brodie.
Brown	Lamont, Macmillan.
Bruce, Brus	Bruce.
Buchan	Cumming.

Family Name.	Connected with Clan.
Buchanan	Buchanan.
Burdon or Bourdon	Lamont.
Burnes, Burns	Campbell of Argyll.
Burnett	Do.
Caddell	Campbell of Cawdor.
Caird	Sinclair.
Calder	Campbell of Cawdor.
Callum	MacLeod of Raasay.
Cambell	Campbell of Argyll.
Cameron	Cameron.
Campbell	Campbell of Argyll.
Cariston	Skene.
Carmichael	Stewart (Appin, Galloway).
Carnegie	Carnegie.
Carnie	Leslie, Skene.
Cattanach	Macpherson.
Caw	MacFarlane.
Chalmers	Cameron.
Cheseholme	Chisholm.
Cheyne	Sutherland.
Chisholm, Chisholme	Chisholm.
Clark or Clarke	Cameron, Mackintosh, Macpherson.
Clarkson	Do. do.
Clerk	Do. do.
Clyne	Sinclair.
Cockburn	Cockburn.
Collier	Robertson.
Colman	Buchanan.
Colquhoun	Colquhoun.
Colson	MacDonald.
Colyear	Robertson.
Combich	Stewart of Appin.
Combie	Mackintosh.
Comrie	MacGregor or MacGrigor.
Comyn	Cumming.
Conacher	MacDougall.
Connall, or Connell	MacDonald.
Conochie	Campbell of Inverawe.
Coulson	MacDonald.
Coutts	Farquharson.
Cowan	Colquhoun, MacDougall.
Cranston	Cranston.
Crauford, Craufurd	Crawford.
Crawford	Do.
Crerar	Mackintosh.
Crookshanks	Stewart of Garth.
Cruickshanks	Do.
Colchone	Colquhoun.
Cumin or Cummin	Cumming.

Family Name.	Connected with Clan.
Cumming . .	. Cumming.
Cumyn . .	. Do.
Cunningham .	. Cunningham.
Currie . .	. MacDonald of Clanranald, Macpherson.
Dallas . .	. Mackintosh.
Dalzell, Dalziel	. Dalzell.
Darroch .	. MacDonald.
Davidson .	. Davidson.
Davie . .	. Do.
Davis, Davison .	. Do.
Dawson . .	. Do.
Denoon, Denune	. Campbell of Argyll.
Deuchar .	. Lindsay.
Dewar . .	. Menzies, Macnab.
Dingwall .	. Munro, Ross.
Dinnes . .	. Innes.
Dis or Dise .	. Skene.
Doles . .	. Mackintosh.
Donachie .	. Robertson.
Donald . .	. MacDonald.
Donaldson .	. Do.
Donillson .	. MacDonald (of Antrim).
Donleavy .	. Buchanan.
Donlevy . .	. Do.
Donnellson .	. MacDonald (of Antrim).
Dougall . .	. MacDougall.
Douglas . .	. Douglas.
Dove . .	. Buchanan.
Dow . .	. Buchanan, Davidson.
Dowall . .	. MacDougall.
Dowe . .	. Buchanan.
Dowell . .	. MacDougall.
Drummond .	. Drummond.
Duff . .	. MacDuff.
Duffie or Duffy	. Macfie.
Duilach . .	. Stewart of Garth.
Dunbar . .	. Dunbar.
Duncan . .	. Robertson.
Duncanson .	. Do.
Dundas . .	. Dundas.
Dunnachie .	. Robertson.
Dyce or Dys .	. Skene.
Edie . .	. Gordon.
Elder . .	. Mackintosh.
Elliot . .	. Elliot.
Erskine . .	. Erskine.
Esson . .	. Mackintosh (Shaw).
Ewan, Ewen .	. MacLachlan.
Ewing . .	. Do.
Farquhar .	. Farquharson.
Farquharson .	. Do.
Federith . .	. Sutherland.
Fergus . .	. Ferguson.

Family Name.	Connected with Clan.
Ferguson, Fergusson .	Ferguson.
Ferries . .	. Do.
Fersen . .	. Macpherson.
Fife, Fyfe .	. MacDuff.
Findlay . .	. Farquharson.
Findlayson .	. Do.
Finlay . .	. Do.
Finlayson .	. Do.
Fleming . .	. Murray.
Fletcher .	. MacGregor.
Forbes . .	. Forbes.
Fordyce . .	. Do.
Foulis . .	. Munro.
France . .	. Stewart (Royal).
Fraser, Frazer .	. Fraser.
Fresell . .	. Fraser.
Freser . .	. Do.
Frezel or Frizel	. Do.
Friseal . .	. Do.
Frisell or Frizell	. Do.
Fullarton Fullerton	. Stuart of Bute.
Galbraith .	. MacDonald, MacFarlane.
Gallie . .	. Gunn.
Garrow . .	. Stewart (Royal).
Gaunson .	. Gunn.
George, Georgeson	. Do.
Gibb, Gibson .	. Buchanan.
Gilbert . .	. Do.
Gilbertson .	. Do.
Gilbride .	. MacDonald.
Gilchrist .	. MacLachlan, Ogilvie.
Gilfillan .	. Macnab.
Gillanders .	. Ross.
Gillespie .	. Macpherson.
Gillies . .	. Do.
Gilmore . .	. Morrison.
Gilroy . .	. Grant of Glenmoriston MacGillivray.
Glen . .	. Mackintosh.
Glennie . .	. Do.
Gordon . .	. Gordon.
Gorrie . .	. MacDonald.
Gow . .	. Macpherson.
Gowan . .	. MacDonald.
Gowrie . .	. Do.
Graeme . .	. Graham.
Graham . .	. Do.
Grahame . .	. Do.
Grant . .	. Grant.
Grassich . .	. Farquharson.
Gray . .	. Stewart of Atholl, Sutherland.
Gregor . .	. MacGregor.
Gregorson .	. MacGregor.
Gregory, Greig	. Do.
Grevsach . .	. Farquharson.
Grier or Grewar	. MacGregor.

Family Name.	Connected with Clan.	Family Name.	Connected with Clan.
Grierson	MacGregor.	Landers	Lamont.
Griesck	MacFarlane.	Lauder	Lauder.
Grigor	MacGregor.	Lean	Maclean.
Gruamach	MacFarlane.	Leckie, Lecky	MacGregor.
Gunn	Gunn.	Lees	Macpherson.
		Lemond	Lamont.
Hallyard	Skene.	Lennie or Lenny	Buchanan.
Hamilton	Hamilton.	Lennox	MacFarlane, Stewart (Royal).
Hardie, Hardy	Farquharson, Mackintosh.	Leslie	Leslie.
Harper, Harperson	Buchanan.	Lewis	Macleod of Lewis.
Hawes, Haws or Hawson.	Campbell.	Leys	Farquharson.
		Limond, Limont	Lamont.
Hawthorn	MacDonald.	Lindsay	Lindsay.
Hay	Hay.	Linklater	Sinclair.
Henderson	Gunn, MacDonald of Glencoe (MacIan).	Livingston	Stewart of Appin.
		Livingstone	Do.
Hendrie, Hendry	MacNaughton.	Lobban	Maclennan.
Hewison	MacDonald.	Logan	Maclennan.
Home, Hume	Home.	Loudoun	Campbell of Loudoun.
Houston	MacDonald.	Love	Mackinnon.
Howison	Do.	Lucas, Luke	Lamont.
Hughson	Do.	Lyon	Farquharson, Lamont.
Huntly	Gordon.		
Hutcheonson	MacDonald.	Mac a' Challies	MacDonald.
Hutcheson, Hutchison	Do.	Macachounich	Colquhoun.
Hutchinson	Do.	MacAdam	MacGregor.
		MacAdie	Ferguson.
Inches	Robertson.	MacAindra	MacFarlane.
Innes, Innie	Innes.	MacAlaster	MacAlister.
Isles	MacDonald.	Macaldonich	Buchanan.
		Macalduie	Lamont.
Jameson, Jamieson	Gunn, Stuart of Bute.	MacAlester	MacAlister.
Johnson	Gunn, MacDonald (MacIan) of Ardnamurchan and of Glencoe.	MacAlister	Do.
		MacAllan	MacDonald of Clanranald, Mac-Farlane.
Johnston, Johnstone	Johnston.		
Johnstoun	Do.	MacAllaster	MacAlister.
		MacAllister	Do.
Kay	Davidson.	MacAlpin, MacAlpine	MacAlpine.
Kean, Keene	Gunn, MacDonald (MacIan), of Ardnamurchan and of Glencoe.	Macandeoir	Buchanan, Macnab.
		MacAndrew	Mackintosh.
Keith	Macpherson, Sutherland.	MacAngus	Macinnes.
Kellie, Kelly	MacDonald.	Macara	MacGregor, Macrae.
Kendrick	MacNaughton.	Macaree	MacGregor.
Kennedy	Cameron, Kennedy.	MacArthur	MacArthur.
Kenneth	Mackenzie.	MacAskill	MacLeod of Lewis.
Kennethson	Do.	MacAslan	Buchanan.
Kerr	Kerr.	MacAulay	MacAulay, Macleod of Lewis.
Kilpatrick	Colquhoun.	MacAuselan	Buchanan.
King	MacGregor.	MacAuslan	Do.
Kinnell	MacDonald.	MacAusland	Do.
Kinnieson	MacFarlane.	MacAuslane	Do.
Kirkpatrick	Colquhoun.	MacAy	Mackintosh (Shaw).
		MacBain	MacBean.
Lachlan	MacLachlan.	MacBaxter	Macmillan.
Lamb	Lamont.	MacBean	MacBean.
Lambie, Lammie	Do.	MacBeath, MacBeth	MacBean, MacDonald, Maclean of Duart.
Lamond, Lamont	Do.		
Lamondson	Do.		

9

Family Name.	Connected with Clan.	Family Name.	Connected with Clan.
MacBeolain	. MacKenzie.	MacCooish	. MacDonald.
MacBheath	. MacBean, MacDonald (Clan Donald, North and South), Maclean of Duart.	MacCook	. MacDonald of Kintyre.
		MacCorkill	. Gunn.
		MacCorkindale	. MacLeod of Lewis.
MacBrayne	. MacNaughton.	MacCorkle	. Gunn.
MacBride	. MacDonald.	MacCormack	. Buchanan.
MacBrieve	. Morrison.	MacCormick	. Maclaine of Lochbuie.
MacBurie	. MacDonald of Clanranald.	MacCorquodale	. MacLeod of Lewis.
MacCaa	. MacFarlane.	MacCorrie	. Macquarrie.
MacCaig .	. Farquharson, MacLeod of Harris.	MacCorry	. Do.
MacCainsh	. Macinnes.	MacCoull	. MacDougall.
MacCaishe	. MacDonald.	MacCowan	. Colquhoun.
MacCall .	. Do.	MacCrae	. Macrae.
MacCallum	. MacCallum.	MacCrain	. MacDonald.
MacCalman	. Buchanan.	MacCraw	. Macrae.
MacCalmont	. Do.	MacCreath	. Do.
MacCamie	. Stuart of Bute.	MacCrie .	. Do.
MacCammon	. Buchanan.	MacCrimmon	. MacLeod of Harris.
MacCammond	. Do.	Maccrouther	. MacGregor.
MacCansh	. Macinnes.	MacCuag	. MacDonald of Kintyre.
MacCardney	. Farquharson, Mackintosh.	MacCuaig	. Farquharson, MacLeod of Harris.
MacCartair	. Campbell of Strachur (Mac-Arthur).	MacCuish	. MacDonald.
		MacCuithein	. Do.
MacCarter	. Do. do.	MacCulloch	. MacDougall, Munro, Ross.
MacCash.	. MacDonald.	MacCunn	. Macqueen.
MacCaskill	. MacLeod of Lewis.	MacCurrach	. Macpherson.
MacCaul	. MacDonald.	MacCutchen	. MacDonald.
MacCause	. MacFarlane.	MacCutcheon	. Do.
MacCaw .	. MacFarlane, Stuart of Bute	Macdade, Macdaid	. Davidson.
MacCay .	. Mackay.	MacDaniell	. MacDonald.
MacCeallaich	. MacDonald.	MacDavid	. Davidson.
MacChlerich	. Cameron, Mackintosh, Mac-pherson.	MacDermid	. Campbell of Argyll.
		MacDiarmid	. Do. do.
MacChlery	. Do. do.	MacDonachie	. Robertson.
MacChoiter	. MacGregor.	MacDonald	. MacDonald.
MacChruiter	. Buchanan.	MacDonell	. MacDonell.
MacCloy	. Stuart of Bute.	Macdonleavy	. Buchanan.
MacClure	. MacLeod of Harris.	MacDougall	. MacDougall.
MacClymont	. Lamont.	MacDowall, MacDowell	Do.
MacCodrum	. MacDonald.	Macdrain	. MacDonald.
MacColl .	. Do.	MacDuff	. MacDuff.
MacColman	. Buchanan.	MacDuffie	. Macfie.
MacComas	. Gunn.	MacDulothe	. MacDougall.
MacCombe	. Macintosh.	MacEachan	. MacDonald of Clanranald.
MacCombich	. Stewart of Appin.	MacEachern	. MacDonald.
MacCombie	. Mackintosh.	MacEachin	. MacDonald of Clanranald.
MacComie	. Do.	MacEachran	. MacDonald.
MacConacher	. MacDougall.	MacEarachar	. Farquharson.
MacConachie	. Robertson.	MacElfrish	. MacDonald.
MacConchy	. Mackintosh.	MacElheran	. Do.
MacCondy	. MacFarlane.	MacEoin	. MacFarlane.
MacConnach	. MacKenzie.	Maceol	. MacNaughton.
MacConnechy	. Campbell of Inverawe, Robert-son.	MacErracher	. MacFarlane.
		MacEwan or	. MacEwan.
MacConnell	. MacDonald.	MacEwen	
MacConochie	. Campbell of Inverawe, Robert-son.	MacFadyen	. Maclaine of Lochbuie.
		MacFadzean	. Do. do.

Family Name.	Connected with Clan.
MacFall	Mackintosh.
MacFarlan	MacFarlane.
MacFarlane	MacFarlane.
MacFarquhar	Farquharson.
MacFater	MacLaren.
MacFeat	Do.
MacFergus	Ferguson.
Macfie or Macfee	Macfie.
MacGaw	MacFarlane.
MacGeachie	MacDonald of Clanranald.
MacGeachin	Do. do.
MacGeoch	MacFarlane.
Macghee, Macghie	Mackay.
MacGibbon	Buchanan of Sallochy, Campbell of Argyll, Graham of Menteith.
MacGilbert	Buchanan of Sallochy.
MacGilchrist	MacLachlan, Ogilvie.
MacGilledow	Lamont.
MacGillegowie	Do.
MacGillivantic	MacDonell of Keppoch.
MacGillivoor	MacGillivray.
MacGillivray	Do.
MacGillonie	Cameron.
MacGilp	MacDonell of Keppoch.
MacGilroy	Grant of Glenmoriston, Mac-Gillivray.
MacGilvernock	Graham of Menteith.
MacGilvra	MacGillivray, Maclaine of Loch-buie.
MacGilvray	MacGillivray.
Macglashan	Mackintosh, Stewart of Atholl.
Macglasrich	MacIvor (Campbell of Argyll), MacDonell of Keppoch.
MacGorrie, MacGorry	MacDonald, Macquarrie.
MacGoun, MacGown	MacDonald, Macpherson.
MacGowan	Do. do.
MacGregor	MacGregor.
MacGreusich	Buchanan, MacFarlane.
Macgrewar	MacGregor.
MacGrigor	Do.
Macgime	Graham of Menteith.
MacGrory	MacLaren.
Macgrowther	MacGregor.
Macgruder	Do.
Macgruer	Fraser.
Macgruther	MacGregor.
MacGuaig	Farquharson.
MacGuaran	Macquarrie.
MacGuffie	Macfie.
MacGuire	Macquarrie.
Machaffie	Macfie.
Machardie, Machardy	Farquharson, Mackintosh.
MacHarold	MacLeod of Harris.
MacHay	Mackintosh (Shaw).
MacHendrie	MacNaughton.
MacHendry	Do.

Family Name.	Connected with Clan.
MacHenry	MacDonald (MacIan) of Glencoe.
MacHowell	MacDougall.
MacHugh	MacDonald.
MacHutchen	Do.
MacHutcheon	Do.
MacIan	Gunn, MacDonald of Ardnamurchan, MacDonald of Glencoe.
Macildowie	Cameron.
Macilduy	MacGregor, Maclean of Duart.
Macilleriach	MacDonald.
Macilreach	Do.
Macilrevie	Do.
Macilriach	Do.
Macilroy	MacGillivray, Grant of Glenmoriston.
Macilvain	MacBean.
Macilvora	Maclaine of Lochbuie.
Macilvrae	MacGillivray.
Macilvride	MacDonald.
Macilwhom	Lamont.
Macilwraith	MacDonald.
Macilzegowie	Lamont.
Macimmey	Fraser.
Macinally	Buchanan.
Macindeor	Menzies.
Macindoe	Buchanan.
Macinnes	Macinnes.
Macinroy	Robertson.
Macinstalker	MacFarlane.
Macintosh	Mackintosh.
Macintyre	Macintyre.
MacIock	MacFarlane.
MacIsaac	Campbell of Craignish, MacDonald of Clanranald.
MacIver or MacIvor	Campbell of Argyll, Robertson of Struan, MacKenzie.
MacJames	MacFarlane.
MacKail	Cameron.
MacKames	Gunn.
Mackay	Mackay.
MacKeachan	MacDonald of Clanranald.
MacKeamish	Gunn.
MacKean	Gunn, MacDonald of Ardnamurchan, MacDonald of Glencoe.
Mackechnie	MacDonald of Clanranald.
Mackee	Mackay.
Mackeggie	Mackintosh.
MacKeith	Macpherson.
MacKellachie	MacDonald.
MacKellaig	Do.
MacKellaigh	Do.
MacKellar	Campbell of Argyll.
MacKelloch	MacDonald.
MacKendrick	MacNaughton.

Family Name.		Connected with Clan.
MacKenrick	.	MacNaughton.
MacKenzie	.	MacKenzie.
MacKeochan	.	MacDonald of Clanranald.
MacKerchar	.	Farquharson.
MacKerlich	.	MacKenzie.
MacKerracher	.	Farquharson.
MacKerras	.	Ferguson.
MacKersey	.	Do.
MacKessock	.	Campbell of Craignish, MacDonald of Clanranald.
MacKichan	.	MacDonald of Clanranald, MacDougall.
Mackie	.	Mackay.
MacKiggan	.	MacDonald.
MacKillican	.	Mackintosh.
MacKillop	.	MacDonell of Keppoch.
MacKim	.	Fraser.
MacKimmie	.	Do.
Mackindlay	.	Farquharson.
Mackinlay	.	Mackinlay.
Mackinley	.	Buchanan.
MacKinnell	.	MacDonald.
Mackinney	.	Mackinnon.
Mackinning	.	Do.
Mackinnon	.	Do.
Mackintosh	.	Mackintosh.
Mackinven	.	Mackinnon.
MacKirdy	.	Stuart of Bute.
MacKissock	.	Campbell of Craignish, MacDonald of Clanranald.
Macknight	.	MacNaughton.
MacLachlan	.	MacLachlan.
Maclae	.	Stewart of Appin.
Maclagan	.	Robertson.
MacLaghlan	.	MacLachlan.
Maclaine	.	Maclaine of Lochbuie.
MacLairish	.	MacDonald.
MacLamond	.	Lamont.
MacLardie, MacLardy		MacDonald.
MacLaren	.	MacLaren.
MacLarty	.	MacDonald.
MacLauchlan	.	MacLachlan.
MacLaughlan	.	Do.
MacLaurin	.	MacLaren.
MacLaverty	.	MacDonald.
MacLaws	.	Campbell.
Maclay	.	Stewart of Appin.
Maclea or Macleay		Livingstone, Stewart.
Maclean	.	Maclean.
MacLehose	.	Campbell.
MacLeish	.	Macpherson.
MacLeister	.	MacGregor.
MacLellan	.	MacDonald.
Maclennan	.	Maclennan.
MacLeod of Harris	.	MacLeod of Harris.
MacLeod of Lewis	.	MacLeod of Lewis.
MacLergain	.	Maclean.

Family Name.		Connected with Clan.
Maclerie	. .	Cameron, Mackintosh, Macpherson.
MacLeverty	.	MacDonald.
MacLewis	.	MacLeod of Lewis, Stuart of Bute.
MacLise	.	Macpherson.
MacLiver	.	MacGregor.
MacLucas	.	Lamont, MacDougall.
MacLugash	.	MacDougall.
MacLulich	.	MacDougall, Munro, Ross.
MacLymont	.	Lamont.
MacMartin	.	Cameron.
MacMaster	.	Buchanan, Macinnes.
MacMath	.	Matheson.
MacMaurice	.	Buchanan.
MacMenzies	.	Menzies.
MacMichael	.	Stewart of Appin, Stewart of Galloway.
Macmillan	.	Macmillan.
MacMinn	.	Menzies.
MacMonies	.	Do.
MacMorran	.	Mackinnon.
MacMunn	.	Stewart.
MacMurchie	.	Buchanan, MacKenzie.
MacMurchy	.	Do. do.
MacMurdo	.	MacDonald, Macpherson.
MacMurdoch	.	Do. do.
MacMurray	.	Murray.
MacMurrich	.	MacDonald of Clanranald, Macpherson.
MacMutrie	.	Stuart of Bute.
Macnab	.	Macnab.
MacNachdan	.	MacNaughton.
MacNachton	.	Do.
MacNaghten	.	Do.
MacNair	.	MacFarlane, MacNaughton.
MacNamell	.	MacDougall.
MacNauchton	.	MacNaughton.
MacNaughtan	.	Do.
MacNaughton	.	Do.
MacNayer	.	Do.
MacNeal	.	MacNeil of Barra, McNeill of Gigha.
MacNee	.	MacGregor.
MacNeil	. .	MacNeil of Barra, McNeill of Gigha.
McNeil of Gigha	.	McNeill of Gigha.
MacNeilage	.	MacNeil.
MacNeiledge	.	Do.
McNeill	.	McNeill of Gigha.
MacNeish	.	MacGregor.
MacNelly	.	MacNeil.
MacNeur	.	MacFarlane.
MacNichol	.	Campbell of Argyll.
MacNicol	.	MacNicol.
MacNider	.	MacFarlane.
MacNie	.	MacGregor.

Family Name.	Connected with Clan.
MacNiel	MacNeil of Barra, McNeill of Gigha.
MacNish	MacGregor.
MacNiter	MacFarlane.
MacNiven	Cumming, Mackintosh MacNaughton.
MacNuir	MacNaughton.
MacNuyer	Buchanan, MacNaughton, MacFarlane.
MacOmie	Mackintosh.
MacOmish	Gunn.
MacOnie	Cameron.
MacOran	Campbell of Melfort.
MacO'Shannaig	MacDonald of Kintyre.
Macoul, Macowl	MacDougall.
MacOurlic	Cameron.
MacOwen	Campbell of Argyll.
MacPatrick	Lamont, MacLaren.
MacPeter	MacGregor.
MacPhail	Cameron, Mackintosh, Mackay.
MacPhater	MacLaren.
MacPhedron	MacAulay.
Macphee or Macphie	Macfie.
MacPheidiran	MacAulay.
Macpherson	Macpherson.
MacPhilip	MacDonell of Keppoch.
MacPhorich	Lamont.
MacPhun	Matheson.
Macquaire	Macquarrie.
Macquarrie	Do.
Macqueen	Macqueen.
Macquey	Mackay.
Macquhirr	Macquarrie.
Macquire	Do.
MacQuistan	MacDonald.
MacQuisten	Do.
Macquoid	Mackay.
Macra	Macrae.
Macrach	Do.
Macrae	Do.
Macraild	MacLeod of Harris.
MacRaith	Macrae, Macilwraith, MacDonald.
MacRankin	Maclean of Coll.
MacRath	Macrae.
Macritchie	Mackintosh.
MacRob	Gunn, MacFarlane.
MacRobb	MacFarlane.
Macrobbie, MacRobie	Robertson.
MacRobert	Do.
MacRorie, MacRory	MacDonald.
MacRuer	Do.
MacRurie, MacRury	Do.
MacShannachan	Do.
MacShimes	Fraser.
MacSimon	Do.
MacSorley	Cameron, MacDonald, Lamont.

Family Name.	Connected with Clan.
MacSporran	MacDonald.
MacSuain	Mcqueen.
MacSwan	Macqueen, MacDonald.
MacSween, MacSwen	Macqueen.
MacSwyde	Macqueen.
MacSymon	Fraser.
MacTaggart	Ross.
MacTary	Innes.
MacTause	Campbell of Argyll.
MacTavish	MacTavish.
MacTear	Ross, Macintyre.
MacThomas	Campbell of Argyll, Mackintosh.
MacTier, MacTire	Ross.
MacUlric	Cameron.
MacUre	Campbell of Argyll.
Macvail	Cameron, Mackay, Mackintosh.
MacVanish	MacKenzie.
MacVarish	MacDonald of Clanranald.
MacVeagh, McVey	Maclean of Duart.
MacVean	MacBean.
MacVicar	MacNaughton.
MacVinish	MacKenzie.
MacVurie	MacDonald of Clanranald.
MacVurrich	Clanranald, Macpherson.
MacWalrick	Cameron.
MacWalter	MacFarlane.
MacWattie	Buchanan of Leny.
MacWhannell	MacDonald.
MacWhirr	Macquarrie.
MacWhirter	Buchanan.
MacWilliam	Gunn, MacFarlane.
Magrath	Macrae.
Malcolm	Malcolm.
Malcolmson	MacLeod of Raasay.
Malloch	MacGregor.
Manson	Gunn.
Marnoch	Innes.
Martin	Cameron, MacDonald.
Masterson	Buchanan.
Matheson, Mathieson	Matheson.
Mathie	Matheson.
Mavor	Innes.
Maxwell	Maxwell.
May	MacDonald.
Means	Menzies.
Meikleham	Lamont.
Mein or Meine	Menzies.
Mengues, Mennie	Do.
Menteith	Graham, Stewart (Royal).
Menzies	Menzies.
Meyners	Do.
Michie	Forbes.
Middleton	Innes.
Mill, Milne	Gordon, Innes, Ogilvie.
Miller	MacFarlane.
Minn, Minnus	MacFarlane.
Mitchell	Innes.

Family Name.		Connected with Clan.	Family Name.		Connected with Clan.
Monach	.	MacFarlane.	Reidfuird	.	Innes.
Monro or Monroe	.	Munro.	Reoch	.	Farquharson, MacDonald.
Monteith	.	Graham, Stewart (Royal).	Revic	.	MacDonald.
Montgomerie	.	Montgomerie.	Riach	.	Farquharson, MacDonald.
Monzie	.	Menzies.	Risk	.	Buchanan.
Moray	.	Murray.	Ritchie	.	Mackintosh.
More	.	Leslie.	Robb	.	MacFarlane.
Morgan	.	Mackay.	Robertson	.	Robertson.
Morison, Morrison	.	Morrison.	Robison, Robson	.	Gunn.
Mowat	.	Sutherland.	Rollo	.	Rollo.
Munn	.	Stewart of Bute.	Ronald	.	MacDonell of Keppoch.
Munro or Munroe	.	Munro.	Ronaldson	.	Do. Do.
Murchie	.	Buchanan, MacDonald, Mac-	Rorison	.	MacDonald.
		Kenzie.	Rose	.	Rose.
Murchison	.	Do. do.	Ross	.	Ross.
Murdoch	.	MacDonald, Macpherson.	Roy	.	Robertson.
Murdoson	.	Do. do.	Ruskin	.	MacCalman (Buchanan).
Murray	.	Murray (Atholl, Tullibardine).	Russell	.	Cumming.
			Ruthven	.	Ruthven.
Napier	.	MacFarlane.			
Neal	.	MacNeil.	Sanderson	.	MacDonell of Glengarry.
Neil or Neill	.	MacNeil.	Sandison	.	Gunn.
Neilson	.	Mackay.	Scott	.	Scott.
Neish	.	MacGregor.	Seton	.	Seton.
Nelson	.	Gunn.	Shannon	.	MacDonald.
Nicholl	.	MacLeod of Lewis.	Shaw	.	Mackintosh.
Nicholson	.	Do.	Sim, Sime, Simon	.	Fraser.
Nicol or Nicoll	.	Do.	Simpson	.	Do.
Nicolson	.	Do.	Sinclair	.	Sinclair.
Nish	.	MacGregor.	Skene	.	Skene, Robertson.
Niven	.	Cumming, Mackintosh, Mac-	Small	.	Murray.
		Naughton.	Smith	.	Clan Chattan, Gow.
Noble	.	Mackintosh.	Sorley	.	Cameron, MacDonald, Lamont.
Norman	.	MacLeod of Harris.	Spalding	.	Murray.
			Spence, Spens	.	MacDuff.
O'Drain	.	MacDonald.	Spittal or Spittel	.	Buchanan.
Ogilvie, Ogilvy	.	Ogilvie.	Sporran	.	MacDonald.
Oliphant	.	Sutherland.	Stalker	.	MacFarlane.
O'May	.	MacDonald.	Stark	.	Robertson.
O'Shaig	.	Do.	Steuart, Stuart	.	Stewart, Royal.
O'Shannachan	.	Do.	Stewart of Appin	.	Stewart of Appin.
O'Shannaig	.	Do.	Stewart of Atholl	.	Stewart of Atholl.
			Stewart of Galloway	.	Stewart of Galloway.
Parlane	.	MacFarlane.	Stewart, Royal	.	Stewart, Royal.
Paterson	.	MacLaren.	Stuart of Bute	.	Stuart of Bute.
Patrick	.	Lamont.	Sutherland	.	Sutherland.
Paul	.	Cameron, Mackintosh, Mackay.	Swan	.	Macqueen.
Peter	.	MacGregor.	Swanson	.	Gunn.
Philipson	.	MacDonell of Keppoch.	Syme	.	Fraser.
Pitullich	.	MacDonald.	Symon	.	Do.
Polson	.	Mackay.			
Purcell	.	MacDonald.	Taggart	.	Ross.
			Tarrill	.	Mackintosh.
Rae	.	Macrae.	Tawesson	.	Campbell of Argyll.
Ramsay	.	Ramsay.	Tawse	.	Farquharson.
Rankin	.	Maclean of Coll.	Taylor	.	Cameron.
Rattray	.	Rattray, Murray.	Thain	.	Innes.
Reid	.	Robertson of Strathloch.			

Family Name.		Connected with Clan.	Family Name.		Connected with Clan.
Thomas	. .	Campbell, Mackintosh.	Vass	. .	Munro, Ross.
Thomason	. .	Campbell, MacFarlane, Mackintosh.	Wallace, Wallis	.	Wallace.
			Warnebald	. .	Cunningham.
Thompson	. .	Campbell of Argyll.	Wass	. .	Munro, Ross.
Thoms	. .	Mackintosh.	Watson	. .	Buchanan.
Thomson	. .	Campbell, Mackintosh.	Watt	. .	Do.
Tolmie	. .	MacLeod of Raasay.	Weaver	. .	MacFarlane.
Tonnochy	. .	Robertson.	Weir	. .	MacNaughton, MacFarlane.
Tosh	. .	Mackintosh.	Wemyss	. .	MacDuff.
Toshach	. .	Do.	Whannell	. .	MacDonald.
Toward, Towart	.	Lamont.	Wharrie	. .	Macquarrie.
Train	. .	MacDonald.	White or Whyte	.	MacGregor, Lamont.
Turner	. .	Lamont.	Williamson	.	Gunn, Mackay.
Tweedie	. .	Fraser.	Wilson	. .	Gunn.
Tyre	. .	Macintyre.	Wright	. .	Macintyre.
Ure	. .	Campbell of Argyll.	Yuill, Yuille	.	Buchanan.
Urquhart	. .	Urquhart.	Yule	. .	Do.

Note.—A great many of the Clan Septs have in modern times adopted Special Tartans, but it has been found impossible to deal with these in the present work.

CHIEF'S ARMS

CHIEF'S BANNER
Carried before, or flown at tent of Chief when he is present.

Chief's Arms and Banner fulfil in the clan the same purposes as Royal Arms do in a Kingdom.

Clansman.

Chief

CAP BADGES

Chieftain

CHIEF'S STANDARD Or Rallying Flag.
Flown at his headquarters at a gathering or such occasion.

CHIEF'S PINSEL
Used in his absence by his Ardtosheador.

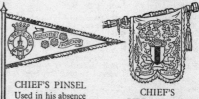

CHIEF'S PIPE BANNER

FLAGS AND BADGES USED AT CLAN GATHERINGS, Etc.

PLANT BADGES OF THE CLANS

(*According to various Authorities*)

Those officially registered marked with an asterisk *

Brodie .	Periwinkle (? Lesser Periwinkle).
Bruce .	Rosemary.
Buchan .	Sunflower.*
Buchanan .	Birch, Blaeberry (Bilberry), Oak.
Cameron .	Cranberry, Crowberry, Oak.
Campbell .	Fir Club Moss, Wild Myrtle.
Chisholm .	Fern.*
Clan Chattan .	Red Whortleberry.*
Colquhoun .	Hazel.*
Cumming .	Cumin (probably really Wheat).
Davidson .	Red Whortleberry (Cowberry).
Drummond .	Holly.*
Farquharson .	Scots Fir.*
Fergusson .	Poplar (*Dunfallandy*); Scots Pine (*Strachur*) ; Rock Rose.
Fletcher .	Scots Pine.
Forbes .	Broom.
Fraser .	Yew
Gordon .	Ivy.*
Graham .	Spurge Laurel.
Grant .	Scots Pine.*
Gunn .	Juniper, Rose Root.
Hay .	Mistletoe.*
Henderson .	Cotton Sedge.
Home .	Broom.
Innes .	Great Bulrush.*
Johnston .	Red Hawthorn.
Kennedy .	Oak.
Lamont .	Crab-Apple Tree.*
Leslie .	Rue.
Lindsay .	Lime Tree, Rue.
Macalister.	Scottish Heather (Ling).
Macalpine.	Scots Pine.
Macarthur .	Wild Thyme.
Macaulay .	Cranberry, Scots Pine (*Ardincaple*).
Macbean .	Boxwood.*
Macdonald .	Scottish Heather.
Macdougall .	" Bell Heath "* (probably Cross-leaved Heath), Cypress.
Macduff .	Oak.
Macfarlane .	Cloudberry, Cranberry.
Macfie .	Crowberry, Oak (*Cameron badges*), Scots Pine.
MacGillivray .	Red Whortleberry.
MacGregor .	Scots Pine.*
Macinnes .	Holly.
Macintyre .	Scottish Heather, White Heather.
Mackay .	Great Bulrush.*
Mackenzie .	Deer's Grass (Heath Club Rush), Variegated Holly.
Mackinnon .	" St. Columba's Flower " (St. John's Wort).
Mackintosh .	Red Whortleberry,* Bearberry.*
Maclachlan .	Rowan.*
Maclaine (Lochbuie)	Blaeberry (Bilberry), Bramble.
Maclaren .	Spurge Laurel.*
Maclean .	Crowberry.
Maclennan .	Furze (Whin).
Macleod .	Juniper (*Macleod of Macleod*) ; Red Whortleberry (*Lewis*).
Macmillan .	Holly
Macnab .	Stone Bramble (Roebuckberry).*
Macnaughton .	Trailing Azalea (Loiseleurea).*
Macneil, McNeill	Dryas, Seaware (Algae), Trefoil.
Macnicol .	Juniper, Trailing Azalea (Loiseleurea).
Macpherson .	White Heather.*
Macquarrie .	Scots Pine.
Macqueen .	Red Whortleberry (*Corryborough*) ; Scottish Heather (*Skye*).
Macrae .	Common Club Moss (Staghorn Moss), Fir Club Moss.
Malcolm .	Rowan berries.
Matheson .	Broom, Holly.
Menzies .	Menzies Heath.*
Munro .	Common Club Moss.
Murray .	Broom, Butcher's Broom ; Juniper (*Atholl*).
Ogilvy .	Evergreen Alkanet, Hawthorn, Ox-tongue.
Oliphant .	Bulrush, Sycamore.
Robertson .	Bracken.*
Rose .	Wild Rosemary (Marsh Andromeda).*
Ross .	Juniper.*
Scott .	Blaeberry.
Seton .	Yew.
Sinclair .	Furze (Whin),* White Clover (Dutch Clover).
Stewart .	Oak.
Sutherland .	Broom, Butcher's Broom, Cotton Sedge.
Urquhart .	Wallflower.*

16

CLAN PLANT-BADGES : NOTES

1. The badge of Clan Alpin is Scots Pine (Scots Fir), that of Clan Chattan is Red Whortleberry (Cowberry), and that of Clan Donald is Scottish Heather (Ling). Boxwood was apparently used on occasion as a substitute for Red Whortleberry.

2. In Scotland " Cranberry " usually means Red Whortleberry.

The plant-badge is apparently the charm, or magic " race-plant " which, with other sacred or saintly relics, was carried beside the " standard " and saintly flags. By clansfolk it is worn pinned behind the silver-crested bonnet or sash-badge brooch.

BRODIE

THIS clan derives its name from Brodie, the home of the chiefs, in Gaelic *Brothach*, a thanage which has belonged to the Brodies from the dawn of history. They are one of the original tribes of Morayshire. Their early charters were destroyed when Brodie House was burnt by Lord Lewis Gordon in 1645. From Malcolm, Thane of Brodie in the reign of Alexander III, the line of chiefs is deduced; and for Michael, son of Malcolm, Thane of Brodie, Robert the Bruce created a barony in 1311. Alexander Brodie of Brodie was, as Lord Brodie, a celebrated judge in the reign of Charles II; and his descendant, Alexander Brodie of Brodie, was Lord Lyon King of Arms, 1727–54. The Lord Lyon's son dying unmarried, he was succeeded as heir of tailzie and Laird of Brodie by his cousin James, son of James Brodie of Spynie, from whom descends the present Brodie of Brodie. Brodie Castle, the seat of the chiefs, is a picturesque old Scottish fortalice. The Brodies of Lethen and the Brodies of Eastbourne in Sussex— of whom Sir Benjamin Brodie, a distinguished surgeon, received a baronetcy in 1834—are the principal cadets of the clan.

Chief : Brodie of Brodie.
Clan Seat : Brodie Castle, Forres.
Plant : Periwinkle.
Memorials : Kirk of Dyke, Moray.

18

CLACKMANNAN TOWER

BRUCE

THE founder was Sir Robert de Brus, a Norman knight. He came to England with William the Conqueror, who granted him vast lands in Yorkshire. His son, Robert, went to Scotland and was made Lord of Annandale by David I, whose great-grand-daughter Isabella married Robert Bruce, 5th Lord of Annandale. Through this marriage their son Robert, 6th Lord of Annandale, Regent of Scotland, inherited a right to the Crown to which he was nominated by Alexander III before the birth of the " Maid of Norway." Robert, 7th Lord, married the Celtic Countess of Carrick ; and their son became that Earl of Carrick who was to wear the Scottish Crown, complete the liberation of Scotland, and be familiarly known as Robert the Bruce. Bruce was born in 1274. He died at Cardross, on the Clyde, in 1329. His body was buried in Dunfermline Abbey, and his heart in Melrose.

The Earl of Elgin bears arms as chief of the Bruces. A Baronetcy of Stenhouse was created in 1629, and of Downhill in 1804.

Chief : Earl of Elgin.
Patronymic : The Bruce.
Clan Seats : Clackmannan Tower, Alloa ; Broomhall, Fife.
Tryst : Lochmabenstone, Annandale.
Plant : Rosemary.

19

BUCHANAN

THE origin of the Buchanans has been traced to one, Gilbert, a Steward of the Earl of Lennox, about the middle of the thirteenth century. The Earl conferred upon Gilbert a part of the lands of Buchanan, from which he took his name. Maurice of Buchanan, his successor, received the same grant from the 6th Earl of Lennox. Maurice married the daughter of Menteith of Rusky, and thus his son became connected with the Royal House. The latter married the sole heiress of the ancient family of Leny. It is said that at the battle of Baugé-en-Anjou, in 1421, Sir Alexander, their eldest son, slew the Duke of Clarence. The former was killed at the battle of Verneuil in 1424, when his second brother, Walter, succeeded to the Buchanan estates, and his third brother to the Leny estates. Walter married Isabel, Countess of Lennox. Their eldest son, Patrick, married the heiress of Killearn and Auchreoch, while Thomas, their youngest son, founded the House of Drumikil, of which the famous historian, George Buchanan, was a descendant. Patrick's son, Walter, married a daughter of Lord Graham, and by her had a younger son who became known as " King of Kippen." Walter, a grandson of Patrick, and founder of the line of Spittal, was twice married. By his second wife he had William, founder of the now extinct line of Auchmar. The principal line became extinct in 1682, when representation was claimed by Buchanan of Auchmar, whose line perished in 1816. The family lands are now possessed by the Duke of Montrose.

Chief : Buchanan of that Ilk.
Clan Seat : Buchanan Castle, Drymen.
Slogan : Clare Innis.
Plant : Bilberry.
Memorials : Clare Innis, in Loch Lomond.

CAMERON

THE Camerons are of pure Celtic ancestry; and Cameron of Lochiel is the chief house of the Clan. Ewen, younger son of Ewen, 13th Chief of Lochiel, was the founder of the house of Erracht. Donald, 2nd of Erracht, joined Prince Charlie at Glenfinnan, where, under Lochiel, he was second in command of the Camerons. His daughter married Cameron of Scamadale, and had a son, Lieutenant Alexander Cameron, who led the Camerons during the last three hours of Waterloo. His eldest son, Sir Alan Cameron of Erracht, K.C.B., went to America and with the 84th, or Royal Emigrants, helped to defend Quebec against Arnold. In 1793 he raised the 79th or Cameron Highlanders. Sir Ewen Cameron of the main line—Lochiel—was one of the greatest cavaliers during the Civil Wars. His loyalty was perpetuated in Donald Cameron of Lochiel, one of Prince Charlie's staunchest friends in 1745. Achnacarry is the seat of the Camerons of Lochiel.

Chief : Cameron of Lochiel.
Patronymic : Mac-Dhomnuil Duibh.
Clan Seat : Achnacarry, Spean Bridge.
Slogan : Chlanna nan Con.
Plant : Oak.
Pipe Music : (1) The Camerons' Gathering. (2) Pibroch of Donnuil Dubh.

21

CAMPBELL OF LOCHOW
DUKE OF ARGYLL

THE name Campbell first appears in 1216, in connection with the Lordship of the Gloume (afterwards Castle-Campbell) near Stirling, and by marriage with Eva O'Duine they became Lords of Lochaw, in Argyll, and chief of Clan Diarmid. The first of importance was Neil Campbell of Lochaw, who, in 1296, was made King Edward's Baillie over the king's lands in Argyll. His great-grandson was created Lord Campbell by James II, and was the first of the family to take the title of Argyll. His grandson, Colin, was made Earl of Argyll in 1457, and Lord of Lorn in 1470. The Marquis of Argyll was the great leader of the Covenanters during the Civil Wars in the reigns of Charles I and Charles II. The 8th Earl was created Duke of Argyll in 1701. The Peerages and estate descended to John, second Duke of Argyll and Earl of Greenwich (died 1743). He was succeeded by his brother, who died without issue, and so the title devolved upon his cousin, General John Campbell of Mamore. Inveraray Castle is the seat of the Campbell Chiefs, whose designation is *MacCailein Mór*.

Chief : Duke of Argyll.
Patronymic : MacCailein Mór.
Clan Seats : Inveraray Castle, Argyll; Ardchonnel Castle, Loch Awe.
Slogan : Cruachan.
Plant : Wild Myrtle.
Memorials : Kilmun Kirk.
Pipe Music : (1) Argyll's Salute. (2) The Campbells are Coming.

CAMPBELL OF BREADALBANE

Chief : Earl of Breadalbane.
Patronymic : Mac-Chailein-'ic Dhonnachaidh.
Clan Seat : Kilchurn Castle, Loch Awe.
Slogan : Cruachan.
Plant : Wild Myrtle.

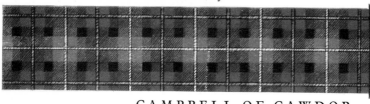

CAMPBELL OF CAWDOR

Chief : Earl of Cawdor.
Clan Seat : Cawdor Castle, Nairnshire.
Plant : Wild Myrtle.
Memorials : Barevon Kirk.

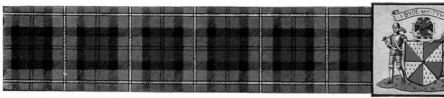

CAMPBELL OF LOUDOUN

CHISHOLM

THE Chisholms are of Lowland origin, but they are virtually Gaelic by descent, an ancestor having married Margaret, the Celtic heiress of Erchless in the Aird. Their Lament is "*Cumha do dh'-Uillean Siosal*" ("Lament for William Chisholm"), and their badge, the Fern. Their ancient stronghold was Erchless Castle in Strathglass, which their descendants still own. A Robert Chisholm, knight, is mentioned in 1369, and a Thomas of Chisholm in 1403. Three of the clan were Bishops of Dunblane in the fifteenth and sixteenth centuries. James Chisholm was Master of the Household to James VI. Mention is made of Alexander Chisholm of Strathglass in 1578, and of John Chisholm of Comer in 1613. In 1608 Lord Balmerino, the Scottish Secretary of State, was taken to task in England for having written to Pope Clement VIII "to obtain a Cardinal's Hat for Chisholm, a Scots man, brother to the Laird of Crouneriggs in Perthshire."

The Chief of the Chisholms is called in Gaelic "*An Siosalach*." The arms of the Chiefs were in 1887 and 1938 confirmed to the heir of line of the baronial house of Comer and Erchless as "Chisholm of Chisholm."

Chief : Chisholm of Chisholm.
Patronymic : An Siosalach (The Chisholm).
Clan Seats : Erchless Castle, and Comer, Strathglass.
Plant : Fern.
Pipe Music : (1) The Chisholm's Salute. (2) Chisholm's March.

COLQUHOUN

THE Colquhouns derive their name from the Barony of Colquhoun in Dunbartonshire. In Alexander II's reign Humphrey Kirkpatrick was granted a charter of these lands of Colchoun. His successor, Ingram, took the surname of Colquhoun of Colquhoun, married the " Fair Maid of Luss," and so acquired that estate. There were three branches of the Colquhouns—of that Ilk, of Kilpatrick, and of Luss. Luss became the chief seat of the family. Sir Humphrey Colquhoun of Luss received other lands from James IV. Sir Humphrey, 17th Laird of Luss, fought against Rob Roy at Loch Lomond. He died in 1715, when the estates and chiefship passed to his daughter and her husband, Grant of Pluscarden. Their son, James Grant, on his succession, took the name of Sir James Colquhoun of Luss. He fell heir to the Grant estates, and, resuming the name of Grant, was succeeded in the Chiefship of Colquhoun and estate of Luss by his second son, Sir Ludovick Grant. He in turn succeeded to the estates of Grant, Luss going to his brother James, who was made a Baronet in 1786, and died the same year. From him descends the present line of chiefs.

Chief : Colquhoun of Luss.
Clan Seats : Rossdhu, Luss, Dunbartonshire ; Luss Barony, Dunbartonshire.
Tryst : Cnoc-ealachan.
Slogan : Cnoc-ealachan.
Plant : Hazel.
Pipe Music : (1) The Colquhouns' March. (2) The Colquhouns' Gathering.

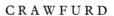

CRAWFURD

THE earliest historic reference to this family is in the charter of William de Lindsay conferred by King William, wherein mention is made of Johannis de Crawford filius Reginaldi. In 1127 there were two knights of this name serving under King David I, Sir John and Sir Gregan; the latter obtained a grant of land from this king in Galloway. The surname is derived from the Barony of Crawford, in Lanarkshire. Members of this family are mentioned in charters of 1170, 1190, 1228, 1230, and 1248. The Arms of Loudoun were quartered by Sir Reginald de Crawford about 1200, on his marriage with Margaret de Loudoun, the heiress of that extensive Barony. Margaret, the daughter of Sir Hugh Crawford, Sheriff of Ayr, married Sir Malcolm Wallace of Elderslie, and became the mother of Sir William Wallace, the hero of Scotland. Sir Reginald Crawford was prominent in the service of both Wallace and Robert the Bruce, and was executed at Carlisle in 1307 for his loyalty to the latter. Crawfurd of Auchinames is chief of the Name, and Crawfurd of Crawfurdland one of the principal branches.

Chief : Crawfurd of Auchinames.
Clan Seat : Auchinames, Lanarkshire.
Plant : Boxwood.

CUMMING

THE Cumins are said to have come from Normandy, but some deduce them from Northumberland. Their home was Badenoch, in the south-eastern wilds of Inverness. John Cumin was slain with Malcolm III at Alnwick in 1093. Sir John, the Red Cumin (Comyn), first Lord of Badenoch, was ambassador to Louis IX of France in 1240, and his son, John, was a competitor for the Scottish Crown, but Edward I of England chose John Baliol to be King of Scotland. This did not prevent Cumin from swearing fealty to the English King. His son, John, called also the Red Cumin (Comyn), succeeded him as Lord of Badenoch. He fought against England in the War of Independence, but quarrelled with Robert Bruce, who stabbed him in the Church of Dumfries. He was the last Lord of Badenoch who was surnamed Cumin. His lands passed to the Earl of Buchan, descended from another Cumin. In revenge the whole clan rose against Bruce, who defeated them. The Earl was outlawed, and his estates were forfeited. His son and successor had no heirs. His kinsman, Jordanus Cumin, is said to have been the ancestor of the Cumins of Culter. The Cumin race is now represented by the Cummings of Altyre and Gordonstoun, Baronets. They have held Altyre in Moray for many generations.

Chief : Cumming of Altyre.

Clan Seats : Altyre, Forres ; Durdargue Castle and Inverallochy Castle, both by Fraserburgh.

Plant : Cummin plant.

27

CUNNINGHAM

THE Cunninghams trace their descent from Warnebald, who settled in the district of Cunningham, Ayrshire, and obtained the manor of that name before 1162, and took his surname from the land. His grandson founded the Cunninghams of Glengarnock, and his grandson was the ancestor of Cunningham of Polmaise. Sir Robert Cunningham swore fealty to King Edward I of England in 1296, and left two sons, from the younger of whom came the Cunninghams of Drumquhassel, Ballindalloch, Balbougie, and Banton. Alexander Cunningham was created Lord Kilmaurs about 1450, and Earl of Glencairn, 1488, but was killed in the same year at the battle of Sauchieburn. The 5th Earl was a great supporter of the Reformation, and when Queen Mary was sent to Loch Leven he went to the chapel at Holyrood and demolished the altar and other things there. After the death of John, 14th Earl, in 1796 without issue, the title became dormant. The Fairlie Cunninghams are the descendants of the second son of the 1st Earl. Cunningham of Corsehill, Baronet from 1673, and representative of the second son of the 3rd Earl of Glencairn, is now regarded as the Chief.

Chief: Cunningham of Kilmaurs.
Clan Seats: Kilmaurs.

DAVIDSON

THE Davidsons are Celtic. Their Clan Pipe Music is " Tulloch's Salute." All that is known of their first Chief is that his name was David. Their home, like that of the Cumins, was in Badenoch. In 1296, along with the Mackintoshes and Macphersons, they met the Camerons in battle at Invernahaven. The Macphersons and MacDhais (Davidsons) disputed priority. Mackintosh favoured the Davidsons, and the Macphersons left the field. The Camerons were victorious. The Macphersons fell upon the Camerons, and defeated them in turn. The Macphersons and the Davidsons now fell out. Reconciliation being useless, it was arranged that thirty men should be selected from each side to fight for the mastery. Robert III was umpire. The battle was fought on the North Inch of Perth in 1396. Only one Davidson was left alive. Since then they have figured but slightly in history. Tulloch, in Ross-shire, was the residence of the Chief. He is the hereditary Keeper of the Royal Castle of Dingwall and owned a small estate of *Davidson* in Easter Ross.

Chief : Davidson of that Ilk or Tulloch.
Clan Seats : Tulloch Castle, Dingwall ; Cantray, Inverness.
Plant : Cranberry.
Pipe Music : Tulloch's Salute.

DOUGLAS

THERE are many legends of the origin of this powerful family, but the first recorded is William de Douglas, who witnessed a charter between 1174 and 1199. Douglasdale in Lanarkshire is the *duthus* of the race, whose chiefs lie buried in Douglas Kirk. His grandson, Sir William " le Hardi," had issue, " the Good " Sir James and Archibald " the Tineman " (*i.e.*, the loser), who was killed at Halidon Hill, leaving a son, William, created 1st Earl of Douglas, who became, through his wife, Earl of Mar. The Earl died in 1384, leaving a son, James, 2nd Earl of Douglas and Mar. " The Good " Sir James, previously mentioned, died in defence of Bruce's heart in Spain in 1330. The 4th Earl was created Duke of Touraine in 1424, and was killed at the battle of Verneuil the same year. The 3rd Duke of Touraine, and 6th Earl of Douglas, was, with his brother, David, lured into Edinburgh Castle and beheaded, 1440. The 7th Earl of Douglas, and 1st Earl of Avondale, was the father of six sons— William, 8th Earl, killed by James II at Stirling, 1452 ; James, 9th and last Earl, forfeited 1455, and died a monk at Lindores in 1488 ; Archibald, Earl of Moray, killed at the battle of Arkinholm, 1455 ; Hugh, Earl of Ormond, beheaded after the same battle ; John, Lord Balveny, beheaded, 1463 ; and Henry, Bishop of Dunkeld. The tartan is illustrated as worn by an officer of the Cameronians (Scottish Rifles).

Chief : Douglas of Douglas.
Patronymic : The Douglas.
Clan Seats : Douglas Castle, Lanarkshire ; Tantallon Castle, East Lothian.
Tryst : Stobhall.
Slogan : A Douglas ! A Douglas !
Memorials : St. Bryde's Kirk, Douglas.
Music : Dumbarton's Drums.

DRUMMOND

THE Drummond Clan derives its name from the lands of Drummond or Drymen, in Stirlingshire. The progenitor of this Clan was Malcolm Beg, Lord of the lands of Drummond and Seneschal of Strathearn in 1225. In 1499 Lord Drummond was in possession of Drymen. The Drummond chiefs were Barons of Cargill and Stobhall on the Tay.

James, 4th Earl of Perth, was Lord Chancellor of Scotland. The "Chevalier" made him Duke of Perth. His eldest son, James, 2nd Duke, was "out" in "the '15," and was attainted. His sons, James and John, 3rd and 4th Dukes, died unmarried. The 5th and 6th Dukes were younger sons of the 1st Duke. Then the Earldom of Perth passed to the Melfort branch. George, son of Léon Drummond, was restored to the Scottish titles of Earl of Perth and Melfort by Queen Victoria in 1853. He died in 1902, when the Melfort title passed to his daughter, Lady Marie Drummond, and the Perth titles to his kinsman, William, 11th Viscount Strathallan. The Clan Pipe March is " *Spaidsearachd Dhiuc Pheairt* " (" Duke of Perth's March ").

Chief : Earl of Perth.

Clan Seats : Castle-Drummond, Crieff ; Stobhall, Perthshire.

Slogan : Gang Warily.

Plant : Holly.

Pipe Music : The Duke of Perth's March.

DUNDAS

SERLE DE DUNDAS is mentioned in the time of King William the Lion. His direct descendant in the fifteenth century, James Dundas, was twice married, and from him are descended the Dundases of Newliston, Duddingston, and Manour. Sir James Dundas of Dundas, great grandson of James Dundas, was twice married, and is the ancestor of the present head of the family, still styled Dundas of Dundas. A representative of the Celtic branch, Robert Dundas, was Lord President of the Court of Session, and was twice married. By his second marriage he had Henry, created Viscount Melville, 1802, ancestor of the present Viscount. By his first marriage the Lord President had a son, who also became Lord President, and was father of Robert, Lord Chief Baron of the Court of Exchequer. His grandson was created a Baronet, 1898. The Dundases of Fingask are descended from James Dundas, who was father of Alexander, who fell at Flodden, 1513, whose direct descendant in the sixth degree, Thomas Dundas, had two sons—Thomas, and Lawrence of Kerse. The last-named Thomas was the ancestor of Charles, created Lord Amesbury, 1832. The above-named Lawrence of Kerse was created a Baronet, 1762, and was father of Sir Thomas, created Baron Dundas of Aske, 1794. His son, Lawrence, 2nd Baron, was created Earl of Zetland, 1838, and his grandson was created Marquis of Zetland, 1892.

Chief : Dundas of Dundas.
Clan Seats : Dundas Castle, South Queensferry ; Inchgarvie, in Firth of Forth.
Plant : Bilberry.

ELLIOT

THE Elliots were an important family in the south of Scotland. The Chief of the clan was of Redheuch, and some other branches of the family were designed as of Larriston, Braidlie, Horsliehill, Arkleton, and Stobs. Of the last-named branch came Gilbert Eliot of Stobs, celebrated in Border history as " Gibbie wi' the gowden garters," who died leaving several sons. William, the eldest, was ancestor of the Baronets of Stobs, now regarded as the principal line of Eliots extant ; also of John Eliot, M.D., Physician to the Prince of Wales, who was created a Baronet, 1778, but died unmarried, 1786 ; and also of the celebrated General George Augustus Eliot, who successfully defended Gibraltar for three years (1779–83) against the whole power of France and Spain. General Eliot was created Lord Heathfield, Baron Gibraltar, 1787, but the title became extinct on the death of his son, Francis, 2nd Baron, 1813. Gavin Eliot of Midlem Mill, 4th son of the above-named Gilbert Eliot of Stobs, was father of Gilbert Eliot, Lord Justice Clerk, created a Baronet, 1700, whose great-grandson, Gilbert, after having been Governor-General of India, was created Earl of Minto, 1813.

Chief : Eliot of Stobs.

Clan Seats : Redheugh, Roxburghshire ; Larriston Tower ; Gilnockie Tower.

ERSKINE

SIR ROBERT ERSKINE of that Ilk, Chamberlain of Scotland, 1350–57, had Thomas, his heir, and Malcolm, ancestor of the Erskines of Kinnoull. Sir Robert's grandson was created Lord Erskine. The 3rd Lord Erskine was succeeded by his son, James, as 5th Lord, who left two sons; the younger, Sir Alexander Erskine of Gogar, had a son, Thomas, created Earl of Kellie, whose line became extinct in 1829; the elder, John, 6th Lord Erskine, was restored the old Celtic Earldom of Mar by Queen Mary. John, 23rd Earl, is well known in connection with the Rising of 1715. In 1875 the House of Lords decided that Walter Henry, 13th Earl of Kellie, had made out his claim to the Earldom of Mar, dated 1565. He died in 1888; and his son, Walter John, became 12th Earl of Mar and 14th Earl of Kellie. The ancient *Celtic* Earldom descended to the heir-female, John F. Goodeve-Erskine, and is the most ancient peerage in Britain. John, Earl of Mar, son of " the Regent Mar," who ruled during the childhood of James VI, had a number of sons. (1) James, the eldest, was created Earl of Buchan. (2) Henry, the second, was the father of James, Lord Cardross, and his descendant became 9th Earl of Buchan. From the 12th Earl the present Earl descends, and from the brother of the 12th Earl come the Lords Erskine. (3) Charles, the third son, was father of another Charles, created a Baronet, whose descendant, the 6th Baronet, inherited the Earldom of Rosslyn from his maternal grandfather, Alexander Wedderburn, Lord Chancellor of England, and his descendants still enjoy this title.

Chief : Earl of Mar and Kellie.
Clan Seats : Alloa Tower, Clackmannan ; Erskine, Renfrewshire.
Plant : Red Rose.

FARQUHARSON

THE Farquharsons are of Celtic origin. Their clan country is Strathdee, in Aberdeenshire. Some of them were originally named Shaw. The offspring of Shaw of Rothiemurchus took the name of Farquharson. In 1645 Farquharson of Invercauld fought at the head of his clan under the famous Marquis of Montrose. The clan was well represented in the army of Prince Charlie in 1745. In 1748 the Laird of Invercauld leased his castle to the Government for ninety years as a military station. The garrison has long been withdrawn. The above-said Laird died in 1750. His son, James, succeeded, and lived until 1806. James left a daughter, Catherine, to whom the insignia of the Farquharson chiefs were confirmed by Lyon Court. She married Captain James Ross, R.N., who adopted the name Farquharson of Invercauld, and to whose line the chiefship descended. The Farquharsons of Inverey have as their most celebrated member the " Black Colonel," famed in Dee-side legend. In 1745 the clan was led by the " Baron Ban," Farquharson of Monaltrie.

Chief : Farquharson of Invercauld.
Patronymic : Mac Fhionnlaidh.
Clan Seats : Invercauld House, and Braemar Castle, Aberdeenshire.
Slogan : Carn-na-cuimhne.
Plant : Scots Fir.

FERGUSSON

THE Fergussons are Celtic. They were long settled in Argyll, where the chiefs of Clann Fhearghuis of Stra-chur were Hereditary Maers of Glenshellich. Fergusson of Dunfallandy has long been Chief of the Fergussons in Atholl. Two of the clan, sons of the Laird of Badyfarow, near Inverury, figured prominently. " Robert the Plotter," concerned in the Ryehouse Plot, escaped detection and died in 1714. James, a Major-General, served under Marlborough at Blenheim. The Fergussons, Baronets of Kilkerran, have held lands in Ayrshire since the reign of Robert I. Sir James Fergusson, 6th Baronet, a distinguished statesman, was killed in the Jamaica earthquake 1906. Adam Ferguson, historian and moral philosopher ; Robert Fergusson, the poet, and Sir William Fergusson, F.R.S., were illustrious members of the clan. " Annie Laurie," heroine of the song, was wife of Fergusson of Craigdarroch. Brigadier-General Ferguson commanded the Highland Brigade at the capture of the Cape of Good Hope.

Chief : Fergusson of Kilkerran.
Patronymic : (Strachur) Clan Fhearghuis Stra-churra.
Clan Seats : Kilkerran Tower, Ayrshire ; Glenshellich in Strachur, Argyll.
Tryst : (Dunfallandy) The Bloody Stone.
Slogan : (Strachur) Clann Fhearghuis gu-brath.

FORBES

THIS clan is Celtic. Their March is "*Cath Glinn Eurainn*" ("The Battle of Glen Eurann"). John of Forbes, first of the name, figured in the reign of William the Lion, when the *duthus* of Forbes (which the race had held from the time when O'Conochar "killed the bear" which made the Braes of Forbes uninhabitable) was feudalised. In 1303 Alexander Forbes defended Urquhart Castle against Edward I, and was slain with the garrison. Alexander Forbes of Forbes was made Lord Forbes about 1442. John, the 6th Lord, was a favourite of James V. The 10th Lord, Alexander, was a General under Gustavus Adolphus. The family is still represented by Lord Forbes, whose seat is Castle Forbes on Donside. The Lords Pitsligo are descendants of William, a son of Sir John Forbes of Forbes, who lived in the reign of Robert II. The 4th Lord was attainted after Culloden. The Baronets of Craigievar spring from Patrick Forbes of Corse, armour-bearer to James III. The Lairds of Culloden are descended from the Forbeses of Tolquhoun, who date from 1420. Sir Alexander Forbes of Tolquhoun saved Charles II's life at the battle of Worcester. This family was ruined by the Darien Scheme. Sir William Forbes, 8th Baronet of Craigievar, succeeded as Lord Sempill in 1884. Their seat is the tall, romantic castle of Craigievar.

Chief : Lord Forbes.
Clan Seats : Castle-Forbes, and Drumminor Castle, Aberdeenshire.
Tryst : Culquhonny Castle.
Slogan : Lonach.
Plant : Broom.
Pipe Music : The Forbes' Gathering.

FRASER OF LOVAT

THE Frasers are French in origin. Clan Pipe Music : "*Cumha Mhic Shimidh*" ("Lovat's Lament"); March : "*Spaidsearachd Mhic Shimidh*" (Lovat's March). Gilbert of Fraser is mentioned in 1109. Sir Simon Fraser of Oliver Castle was done to death by Edward I. Hugh was the first designed of Lovat, and from him descends the "Clan Fraser of Lovat." Hugh, second of Lovat, was made a Baron about 1460. Hugh, 3rd Lord, fell fighting with the MacRonalds near Lochlochy in 1544. Hugh, 9th Lord, died, leaving only daughters. Amelia, the eldest, married a Mackenzie. He became a Jacobite in 1714, which enabled Simon, the heir-male, to bring the clan in allegiance to the Government, obtain pardon for numerous crimes, and become 11th Lord. In 1746 his title was attainted, and he was beheaded. The title was revived in 1837, and passed to Thomas Fraser of Streichen and Lovat, from whom is descended the present Lord Lovat. His seat is Beaufort Castle on the old estate of Lovat. Another branch of the family is the Frasers (Baronets) of Ledclune ; while the House of Fraser of Philorth is represented by Lord Saltoun.

Chief : (of the whole Name) Lord Fraser.
Patronymic : (Lovat) Mac Shimidh.
Clan Seats : Castle-Fraser, Sauchen ; Caernbulg Castle, Philorth, Aberdeenshire ; Beaufort Castle, Beauly.
Slogan : A' Mhor Fhaich.
Plant : Yew.
Memorials : Rathen Kirk.
Pipe Music : The Frasers' Salute.

GORDON

THE Gordons had their origin in the Border, deriving their name from Gordon in Berwickshire. They acquired power in the North from their exploits in the Scottish War of Independence. They rose to power in the person of Sir Adam Gordon, the friend of Wallace, and to whom Bruce granted the lands of Huntly or Strathbogie. He fell at Halidon Hill in 1333. Alexander, 3rd Earl of Huntly, fought at Flodden. George, 6th Earl, was created a Marquis in 1599. George, 4th Marquis, was made Duke of Gordon in 1684. The Dukedom lapsed in 1836, and the Marquisate went to the Earl of Aboyne. The Earls of Aberdeen are descended from Patrick Gordon of Methlie, who fell in battle at Arbroath in 1445. Ten Baronetcies pertain to this clan : Gordonstoun, Cluny, Lismore, Lochinvar, Park, Dalpholly, Earlstoun, Embo, Halkin, Niton. Two regiments have been raised from it. The 92nd, or Gordon Highlanders, raised in 1794, and the old 75th and 92nd linked together, are now the Gordon Highlanders. The Marquis of Huntly is chief of the Gordon clan.

Chief : Marquis of Huntly.

Patronymic : The Gordon.

Clan Seats : Huntly Castle, Huntly ; Aboyne Castle, Aboyne, Aberdeenshire.

Tryst : Standing Stone of Strathbogie (Huntly).

Slogan: An Gordonach.

Plant : Rock Ivy.

Memorials : Elgin Cathedral.

Pipe Music : (1) The Cock o' the North. (2) Marquis of Huntly's Farewell.

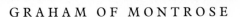

GRAHAM OF MONTROSE

S IR WALTER SCOTT says, " few families can boast of more historical renown than that of Graham." Their origin is wrapped in the mists of antiquity, but tradition has it that the Grahams are descended from a famous warrior who breached the Roman Wall in 420, and won it the name of Graham's Dyke. The first recorded appearance of the name is William of Graham, one of the witnesses to David I's Holyrood Charter (1143–47). He obtained the lands of Abercorn and Dalkeith. His grandson, David Graham, acquired from William the Lion, before 1214, certain lands near Montrose. Under Alexander I his son obtained the lands of Dundaff and Strathearn from the Earl of Dunbar, and those of Strathblane and Mugdock from the Earl of Lennox. Sir William Graham of Dundaff, chief of Clan Graham, during the reign of James I married, as his second wife, May Stewart, the second daughter of King Robert III. Patrick, his eldest grandson, was in 1445 raised to the peerage as Lord Graham, in recognition of his gallantry in the field and his services as a Lord of Regency during the minority of James III. William, 3rd Lord Graham, was in 1504 created Earl of Montrose, the title being derived from the lands of " Auld Montrose." James, 5th Earl, was the celebrated Marquis of Montrose, the Marquisate being created in his favour in 1644. James, 4th Marquis, was created Duke of Montrose in 1707. From him is descended the present Duke, Chief of the clan.

Chief : Duke of Montrose.
Patronymic : An Greumach-Mor (The Graham).
Clan Seats : Mugdock Castle, Stirlingshire ; Dundaff Hills, West Stirlingshire.
Plant : Spurge Laurel.
Memorials : Inchmahome Priory.
Pipe Music : Raon Ruraidh (March).

40

GRAHAM OF MENTEITH

MALISE GRAHAM, a junior grandson of Sir Patrick the Graham of Dundaff, ancestor of the ducal house of Montrose, married Euphemia Stewart, Countess Palatine of Strathearn, of which dignity James I deprived them, but created Malise Earl of Menteith in 1427. William, 7th Earl and Lord Justice General, established his right as Earl Palatine of Strathearn in 1630 ; but this aroused such envy that his confirmation was recalled, and the arms of Strathearn were ordered to be " dashed out of his windows." He was created Earl of Airth in 1633. His son, Lord Kilpont, was murdered under dramatic circumstances by Stewart of Ardvoirlich, as recorded in Scott's *Legend of Montrose.* William Graham, Lord Kilpont's son, succeeded his grandfather as Earl of Airth and Menteith, but little was left of the estates. Since his death in 1694, the Earldoms of Airth and Menteith and Strathearn have been dormant. There are many cadets of the Grahams of Menteith, of whom the most celebrated are the Grahams of Gartmore and Ardoch, descending from the fifth son of the 1st Earl, and of which house the Scottish patriot, R. B. Cunningham Graham of Gartmore and Ardoch, M.P., was lately the representative.

Chief : Graham of Gartmore.
Clan Seat : Inchtalla Castle, Lake of Menteith.
Plant : Spurge Laurel.
Memorials : Inchmahome Priory.

GRANT

THE Grants are Celtic. "*Stad, Chreag Ealachaidh*" ("Stand Fast, Craigellachie") is their slogan. They are of the same stock as the MacGregors, and their location has always been Strathspey. Sir Laurence Graunt, Sheriff of Inverness (1249–58), acquired the greater part of Strathspey. Sir Ian Ruadh Grant, Chief of the clan, in 1381 married Matilda de Glencairnie; and for his descendant, John, *Am Bard Ruadh*, the lands of Freuchie were created a feudal barony. His successor, *Sheumas nan Creach*, was a friend of Mary Queen of Scots. From John Grant of Freuchie and Grant, a strong supporter of James IV, are descended the Chiefs of Grant and Strathspey, and the Baronets of Corrimony and of Glenmoriston. James Grant of Grant and his son Ludovick were in the clan fight at the Haughs of Cromdale. Glenmoriston fought for Prince Charlie at Culloden. There are three Baronetcies—Dalvey, 1688; Monymusk, 1705; and Ballindalloch, 1838. Many of the Glenmoriston Grants were banished to Barbadoes after "the '45." They have a distinct tartan. The clan raised the Grant or Strathspey Fencibles in 1793, and the "old 97th" in 1794. The first was disbanded in 1799, and the other was drafted into other Highland regiments in 1795. Lord Strathspey is the Chief of the clan.

Chief : Lord Strathspey.
Patronymic : An Granntach.
Clan Seat : Castle-Grant, Grantown-on-Spey.
Tryst : Upper Craigellachie.
Slogan : Stand Fast, Craigellachie.
Plant : Scots Fir.
Memorials : Duthil Kirk.
Pipe Music : (1) The Grants' Gathering. (2) Stand Fast Craigellachie March.

GUNN

ORIGINALLY this clan was Norse. The founder of the family was said to be a pirate who settled at Ulbster in Caithness. His descendants and the Keiths were continually at war with each other. The daughter of Lachlan Gunn was carried off by a Keith to Ackergill, where she threw herself from the top of the tower. In 1426 the two clans fought a desperate and indecisive battle near Thurso. Another encounter occurred on the Muir of Tannach in 1438 ; the Gunns were defeated. In 1464 the clans agreed to settle in a friendly way. The Keiths treacherously attacked and cut the Gunns to pieces. The greater part of the clan afterwards migrated to Sutherland. From Henry Gunn the Hendersons of Caithness are descended. Sir William Gunn of this clan fought valiantly under Gustavus Adolphus. In 1636, on the Plains of Weslock, he was chiefly instrumental in defeating the Austrians. Charles I knighted him for bravery. The Chiefs of Clan Gunn were Hereditary Coroners of Caithness, and the official Badge of the Coroner was a great buckle of Celtic design.

Chief : dormant.
Patronymic : Am Braisteach Mor.
Clan Seat : Clyth Castle, Caithness
Plant : Juniper or Rose Root.
Pipe Music : The Gunns' Salute.

HAMILTON

THE founder of this family was Walter, son of Gilbert de Hameldone, to whom Bruce gave the Barony of Cadzow in Lanarkshire, celebrated as the home of the old white Caledonian cattle. Sir James the Hamilton, Lord of Cadzow under James II, was in 1445 created Lord Hamilton. By his wife, Princess Mary, sister of James III, he had James, 2nd Lord, created Earl of Arran, 1502, whose son James, 2nd Earl, the Regent Arran of Mary Queen of Scots' childhood, founded Hamilton Palace, and was declared by Parliament, after her, next heir to the throne. His son John became Marquis of Hamilton, 1599, and James, 3rd Marquis, became Duke of Hamilton, 1643. William, 2nd Duke, died in defence of Charles II at Worcester, 1651. His daughter, Anne, became Duchess of Hamilton. Her son James, 4th Duke, patriotically opposed the Union, 1707, and was shortly after killed by an English peer, Lord Mohun. William, 12th Duke, was in 1864 confirmed by Napoleon III in the French duchy of Chatelherault. Alfred, 13th Duke, after the demotion of Hamilton Palace, removed the seat of the chiefs to Dungavel in their Lordship of Avon. The Duke of Hamilton is Chief of the family, and Hereditary Keeper of the Palace of Holyroodhouse.

Chief : Duke of Hamilton.
Clan Seat : Cadzow Castle.
Plant : Bay Leaves.
Memorials : Hamilton Ducal Mausoleum.

SERVA · JUGUM

HAY

WILLIAM DE HAYA, who flourished about 1170, is said to have been the father of two sons, of whom the younger, Robert, was ancestor of the Marquises of Tweeddale. From the elder son, William, came the house of Erroll, and his descendant, Sir William Hay, was created Earl of Erroll in 1453. The Hays of Erroll hold the office of Hereditary Constable of Scotland, this title having been conferred in 1314 by King Robert Bruce on the grandfather of the 1st Earl. The 4th Earl fell at Flodden in 1513, and the 13th Earl, dying unmarried in 1717, was succeeded by his sister as Countess of Erroll. But on her death in 1758, without issue, the title went to James Boyd, son and heir of the 4th (and attainted) Earl of Kilmarnock, by his wife, Ann Livingstone, who was the daughter and heiress of the Earl of Linlithgow and Callander, and his wife, Margaret Hay, sister of the above-mentioned Countess of Erroll. On succeeding to the title James Boyd changed his name to Hay, in accordance with clan law ; and his descendants succeeding to the Earldom have been continual Chiefs of the Clan Hay.

Chief : Countess of Erroll.

Patronymic : MacGaradh Mor.

Clan Seats : Mote of Erroll, Perthshire ; Old Slains Castle, Aberdeenshire.

Slogan : A Hay ! A Hay ! A Hay !

Plant : Mistletoe.

Memorials : Inchaffray Abbey.

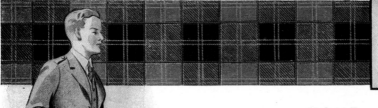

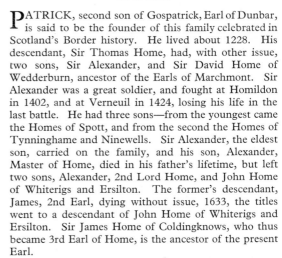

HOME

PATRICK, second son of Gospatrick, Earl of Dunbar, is said to be the founder of this family celebrated in Scotland's Border history. He lived about 1228. His descendant, Sir Thomas Home, had, with other issue, two sons, Sir Alexander, and Sir David Home of Wedderburn, ancestor of the Earls of Marchmont. Sir Alexander was a great soldier, and fought at Homildon in 1402, and at Verneuil in 1424, losing his life in the last battle. He had three sons—from the youngest came the Homes of Spott, and from the second the Homes of Tynninghame and Ninewells. Sir Alexander, the eldest son, carried on the family, and his son, Alexander, Master of Home, died in his father's lifetime, but left two sons, Alexander, 2nd Lord Home, and John Home of Whiterigs and Ersilton. The former's descendant, James, 2nd Earl, dying without issue, 1633, the titles went to a descendant of John Home of Whiterigs and Ersilton. Sir James Home of Coldingknows, who thus became 3rd Earl of Home, is the ancestor of the present Earl.

Chief : Earl of Home.
Clan Seat : Home Castle, Berwickshire.
Slogan : A Home ! A Home ! A Home !
Plant : Broom.

INNES

THIS Clan derives its name from the Barony of Innes, "all the lands betwixt Spey and Lossie," granted by Malcolm IV to Berowald of Innes at Christmas 1160, after his conciliation with Somerled, Lord of the Isles. From Berowald descended a long line of Chiefs (of whom Sir Robert Innes of that Ilk, 1st Baronet, received Charles II on his landing at Speymouth, 1650), Sir James, 6th Baronet, becoming in 1805 5th Duke of Roxburghe, and his son being in 1837 created Earl Innes. From Walter of Innermarkie, second son of Sir Robert Innes of that Ilk, sprang the Baronets of Balveny and Edingight (created 1628), and the Baronets of Coxton (created 1686). From Robert of Drainie came the Inneses of Drumgask and Balnacraig, of whom was Father Lewis Innes, the Jacobite Secretary of State. These branches were all loyal to the House of Stewart, as were the Inneses of Cathlaw, related to the millionaire Mitchell-Inneses of Stow. The arms shown here have been those of the Royalist and Jacobite line of Innes of Balveny. Innes House and Coxton Tower, both near Elgin, are outstanding examples of Scots architecture. John Innes, Bishop of Moray, 1407–14, rebuilt the tower of Elgin Cathedral after its destruction by the Wolf of Badenoch in 1390.

Chief : Innes of that Ilk.
Clan Seats : Innes, by Elgin, Moray and Motte of Innes, Moray ; Edder-Innes, Garmouth.
Tryst : Lawhill (" Loch-hill ") of Innes.
Slogan : An Innes ! An Innes ! An Innes !
Plant : Great Bulrush.
Memorials : Elgin Cathedral (S. Transept).
Pipe Music : (1) Duke of Roxburghe's March. (2) Balvenie Castle, Strathspey.

47

JOHNSTON

THE Johnston family belong to Dumfries, and the original John who had a " toun " or " dwelling " there, lived in the twelfth century. His descendant in the sixth generation was Sir Adam Johnston of that Ilk, who died in 1455. From his eldest son, John, descended the Lords Johnston, Earls of Hartfell, and Marquesses of Annandale. George, the last Marquess, died in 1792. Another son of Sir Adam was Gilbert, the first of the family of Johnstons of Elphinstone. His descendant, Samuel, was created a Baronet. The Johnstons of Westerhall are descended from a Matthew Johnston, also supposed to be a son of Sir Adam. His descendant was created a Baronet in 1700. The present Baronet of Westerhall and also Lord Derwent belong to this family. The 5th Baronet's daughter was created Countess of Bath. The North Country Johnstons claim descent from the Dumfriesshire family. The Johnstons of Gretna and Newbie have not yet been connected with the principal house. There were also Johnstons of Elsieheills, Lockerbie, Beirholm, Sheens, and Warriston, and to the last belongs Sir Archibald Johnston, Lord Warriston, executed in 1663. The Johnstons of Caskieben were not officially recognised as " of that Ilk " from a place in the Garioch, quite distinct from the seat of the Johnston chief in Annandale, " Laird of Johnston " and later Lord Johnson in the peerage, whose arms are shown as chief.

Chief : Johnston of that Ilk and Annandale.
Clan Seat : Lochwood Tower, Dumfries.
Plant : Red Hawthorn.

KENNEDY

IN the twelfth century lived Duncan de Carrick in Ayrshire, whose descendant in the sixth degree was Sir John Kennedy of Dunure, father of Gilbert, whose son, Sir James, married a daughter of King Robert III. His son, Gilbert, was created Lord Kennedy about 1452. The 3rd Lord was created Earl of Cassilis (Cassels) about 1509, but was killed with most of the Scottish nobility at Flodden, 1513. The 3rd Earl died in 1558, it is supposed by poison, leaving two sons—Gilbert, 4th Earl, and Thomas of Cullean. From the 4th Earl descended the 5th, 6th, and 8th, the last of whom died in 1759. On his death, William Douglas, Earl of Ruglen and March, claimed the titles as heir-general, but was not successful. On the death, unmourned, in 1792, of David, 10th Earl, a descendant of Thomas of Cullean previously mentioned, the titles went to a descendant of the second son of Sir Alexander Kennedy, son of Thomas of Cullean. This was Archibald Kennedy, who became 11th Earl, and his son was created Marquis of Ailsa in 1806. Culzean Castle, their principal but not the chiefly seat, is now held by the National Trust for Scotland.

Chief : Marquess of Ailsa.
Clan Seats : Cassillis House, Maybole ; Culzean Castle, Ayrshire.
Plant : Oak.

49

KERR

JOHN KERR of the Forest of Selkirk, living 1357, was father of Henry, Sheriff of Roxburgh, whose son, Robert, was father of Andrew of Auldtounburn. This Andrew Kerr had three sons. From the youngest came the Kerrs of Gateshaw, and from the second the Kerrs of Linton. The eldest son was father of Walter of Cessford, who had two sons. From the younger descended the Kerrs of Dolphinstoun, Littledean, and Morriston. The elder, Sir Robert of Caverton, died in his father's lifetime, leaving two sons—George of Faudonside, and Sir Andrew, who succeeded his grandfather in Cessford. Sir Andrew had three sons. From the first are descended the Dukes of Roxburgh. The second had a son, Mark, who was created Earl of Lothian, 1606, but the title became extinct in 1624. The third son of Sir Andrew of Cessford was ancestor to Sir Thomas of Ferniehirst, whose son by his first marriage, was created Lord Jedburgh, 1622, and by his second marriage had two sons—Sir James, whose son became Lord Jedburgh, and Robert, Earl of Somerset, 1613. Robert of Ancrum, uncle of above-named Sir Thomas, had two grandsons—William, from whom descended the Kerrs of Linton, and Sir Robert, created Earl of Ancrum, 1633, and was succeeded in the title by the son of his second marriage, Charles ; his grandson by his first marriage, Robert 4th Earl of Lothian, also succeeded to the Earldom of Ancrum, and was created Marquess of Lothian, 1701. His direct descendant is the present Marquess of Lothian.

Chief : Marquess of Lothian.
Clan Seat : Ferniehirst Castle, Jedburgh.
Plant : Moss Myrtle.
Memorials : Newbattle Abbey.

LAMONT

THE Lamonts are a Celtic family. The old seat of the Chief was Castle Toward. This was changed to Ardlamont, between the Kyles of Bute and Loch Fyne, which was the seat of the Chiefs until the close of the nineteenth century. The surname of the clan is from one Lauman. A Duncan MacLamont seems to have been Laird of Lamont in Robert III's reign. There were also Lamonts of Inverin, the greater part of whose lands was appropriated by the Campbells. John Lamont of Lamont married Lady Jean Campbell, daughter of the Earl of Argyll who fell at Flodden. The Lamonts fought under Montrose at Philiphaugh in 1645. Attacked by the Campbells, they bravely defended themselves in the Castle of Toward, but had to surrender, and were all put to the sword by the victors. In 1685–86 the Laird of Lamont and Archibald Lamont of Silvercraigs were Commissioners in the Parliament at Edinburgh. There were also Lamonts of Willowfield. In course of time the estates passed to Dougal Lamont of Stilaig. His eldest daughter was married to John Lamont of Kilfinnan, and their eldest son succeeded to the estate and chiefship in right of the maternal line.

Chief : Lamont of that Ilk.
Patronymic : Mac Laomuinn.
Clan Seats : Ardlamont, Argyll ; Castle Toward.
Plant : Crab Apple.
Pipe Music : Lamont's Welcome.

LESLIE

THIS clan derives its name from Leslie in the Garioch, in Aberdeenshire, which their progenitor had clearly acquired by settlement, and Malcolm, son of Bartolf got a feudal charter of *his* lands about 1214, which acknowledges they were already " his," evidently held allodially. Sir Andrew Leslie of that Ilk was one of the Scottish nobles who signed the letter to the Pope, declaring that while one hundred Scotsmen lived, they would never yield to England. George, 10th of Leslie, was 1st Earl of Rothes. The 3rd Earl fell at Flodden. John, 7th Earl of Rothes was a zealous adherent of Charles II, and was with him in exile. After the Restoration he was Lord High Chancellor. In 1680 he was created Duke of Rothes. Sir Alexander Leslie (1st Earl of Leven, 1641) was a renowned Field-Marshal under Gustavus Adolphus. He afterwards led the armies of the Covenant. His title is now united with that of Melville. Sir David Leslie (1st Lord Newark, 1660) was another veteran of Gustavus's wars. The title has been dormant since 1791. Sir Patrick Leslie of Pitcairlie was made Lord Lindores in 1600. This title has been dormant since 1775. The Earls of Rothes, Chiefs of the clan, still hold Rothes Castle on the Spey. The tartan is illustrated as worn by an officer of the King's Own Scottish Borderers.

Chief : Earl of Rothes.

Clan Seats : Leslie Castle, Aberdeenshire ; Rothes Castle, Moray ; Ballinbreich Castle, and Leslie-on-Leven House, Fife.

Plant : Rue.

LINDSAY

RANDOLPH, Sire de Toeny, living 1018, descendant of Ivar, Jarl of the Uplanders, is said to be the ancestor of this family. From him descended Sir David Lindsay of Crawford, living 1340, who had two sons : (1) Sir Alexander of Glenesk, father of David, created Earl of Crawford, 1398 ; and (2) Sir William of The Byres. The 5th Earl was created Duke of Montrose, 1488. His son, John, 6th Earl, did not succeed to the Dukedom, and fell at Flodden, 1513. The 8th Earl, in consequence of his son's disgraceful behaviour, resigned his title to the King, who re-granted it, with the provision that at his death it should go to his cousin, David of Edzell. Accordingly, on the 8th Earl's death, David of Edzell became 9th Earl ; but he generously obtained a re-grant of the title to David, grandson of the 8th Earl, who became 10th Earl, 1558. On the death of the 16th Earl the title went to the Lindsays of The Byres, passing over the Edzell family. David, 9th Earl of Crawford, left two sons : (1) Sir David of Edzell, whose line failed, 1744 ; and (2) John of Balcarres, father of David, created Lord Lindsay of Balcarres, 1633, whose son, Alexander, was created Earl of Balcarres, 1651. This Earl's grandson, James, left two sons, one of whom, Alexander, 6th Earl., became 23rd Earl of Crawford, 1808, on the failure of the direct line of the Lindsays of The Byres, and his descendant is the present Earl of Crawford and Balcarres, whose seat is Balcarres, Fife.

Chief : Earl of Crawford.
Patronymic : Le Lindesay.
Clan Seats : Balcarres, Colinsburgh ; and Ochteruter-struther Castle, Fife ; Finhaven Castle, Angus.
Plant : Linden Tree.
Memorials : Crawford Priory, Fife.

MACALISTAIR

THIS clan was the first that branched off from the main Clan Donald stem, probably early in the thirteenth century. Alister Mòr, Lord of the Isles and Kintyre, in 1284, was the founder. He opposed Bruce, who shut him up in Dundonald Castle on the Clyde. He died there, and his estates were given to his brother, Angus Mòr, one of Bruce's supporters. As Lords of the Isles, the dynasty was overthrown by James IV, and the MacAlisters became a distinct clan at Ardpatrick in South Knapdale, Argyllshire. Their descendants were called *Vic-Ian-Dhu*. Mention is made of Vic-Ian-Dhu MacAlister of Loup in 1515. The MacAlisters fought on the side of Montrose at Inverlochy in 1645. Argyll dissuaded Hector, their Chief, from being present. Hector's son, Godfrey, married a daughter of Sir Robert Montgomerie of Skelmorlie. Their son, Alexander MacAlister of Loup, fought for Dundee at Killiecrankie in 1689. His brother, Charles, married a daughter of Lamont of that Ilk. His grandson, Charles, added (by marriage) the Somerville Arms to his own. Dying in 1847, he was succeeded by his son, Charles Somerville MacAlister, who died in 1891. He was succeeded by his son, Lieut.-Colonel Charles Somerville MacAlister. The present Chief is the MacAlistair of the Loup and Kennox. Sir William Alexander of Menstrie, created Earl of Stirling, founded Nova Scotia and induced James I to found the Baronets of Nova Scotia.

Chief : MacAlistair of the Loup.
Patronymic : Mac Iain Duibh.
Clan Seat : Menstrie Castle, by Stirling.
Plant : Heather (ling).

54

MACALPINE

THE Clan MacAlpine is Celtic. It is claimed that this clan is a Royal one, and that it is the most ancient in the Highlands. Some records indicate that for twenty-five generations Kings of Scotland were of the Mac-Alpine lineage. The ancient crest was a boar's head, the war cry being *Cumbrich Bas Ailpein*—"Remember the death of Alpin." The Alpin alluded to was King Alpin, murdered by Brudus after the defeat of the Scots by the Picts near Dundee in 834. The traditional home of the MacAlpines was Dunstaffnage, near Oban, Argyll. Some historians assign an Alpinian origin to the MacGregors, Mac-kinnons, Macnabs, Grants, Macquarries, and others, and group them together under the name of *Siol Ailpein*. Doubt has been cast on the accuracy of this origin. The Mac-Gregor clan seems to have been the principal one. This would seem vouched for in the MacGregor motto, "*Is Rioghail mo Dhream*" ("My race is Royal"), though later writers question this. Unfortunately most of the foregoing is vague tradition. No MacAlpine has recorded arms or pedigree. The "Clan Alpine" was to have been a confederacy consisting of Grants, Macgregors, and others to counterbalance the Clan Chattan, but they disagreed on various matters at the inaugural meeting, so the confederation never materialised.

MACARTHUR

THE MacArthurs are Celts. A tribe of this clan were
hereditary pipers to the MacDonalds of the Isles.
MacArtair aided Robert the Bruce, from whom he
received the forfeited estates of MacDougall. John
MacArtair held princely state ; but this ended when a
later MacArtair was beheaded by James I, and his lands
were forfeited. In later days the MacArthurs gained
part of Strachur, in Cowal, Argyllshire, and also owned
a portion of Glenfalloch and Glendochart. The family
seat of the MacArthurs of Tir-a-cladich was on Loch
Awe side. The title *Mac-ic-Artair* suggests that Tir-a-
cladich was a cadet of the main MacArtair line.

Chief : MacArthur of Tirracladdich.
Patronymic : Mac-ic-Artair.
Clan Seat : Tirracladdich on Loch Awe, Argyll.
Slogan : Eisd ! O Eisd !
Plant : Wild Thyme.

MACAULAY

THE MacAulays are Celtic in origin. Their chief seat was Ardincaple, in Row, Dunbartonshire. Ardincaple was probably built in the twelfth century. At one time they dwelt in Kintail and some think they belong to the Lennox family. It is said the original name was Ardincaples of that Ilk, until they took the name of a chief called Aulay. Aulay is mentioned in various charters by Malduin, Earl of Lennox, whose death took place the beginning of the reign of Alexander III. Aulay was the Earl's brother. His son and successor, Duncan, or MacAulay, Knight, is also named in the Earl's charters. Subsequently, in 1587, Sir Aulay MacAulay is enrolled as among the chief vassals of the Earl of Lennox. A branch of the clan went to Antrim, in Ireland, and acquired the lands of Glenerm. The last portion of the clan territory passed out of the hands of the 12th Chief in 1767, when Ardincaple was sold to the Duke of Argyll. Lord Macaulay, the historian and essayist, belonged to the Clan MacAulay of Lewis, first on record in 1610, and a separate clan from the MacAulays of Ardincaple.

Chief : Macaulay of Ardincaple.
Clan Seat : Ardincaple Castle, Row, Dunbartonshire.
Plant : Scots Fir.

MACBAIN

THIS is a Celtic clan, and the name can be traced for four centuries. They formed one of the branch-clans of the Clan Chattan. MacBain of Kinchyle is the chief line and the early Chiefs might seem to have been Sword-bearers to the MacGillichattan and to have come North with Eva the Heretrix of Clan Chattan. Their Chief in the early fourteenth century was *Bean MacMilmor*. A division of the clan was " out " with Lochiel in " the '45," but on all other occasions they have mustered under the banner of Macintosh, and have acknowledged him as their high Chief. The Chief of the clan was a Major in the Macintosh battalion of Prince Charlie's army. Father and son fought for the Prince. At Culloden Major Gillies MacBean, a man of gigantic stature, placed himself in the gap of a wall, and mowed down the English with his broadsword. Thirteen, including Lord Robert Kerr, fell to his hand before his enemies closed upon him, then, with his back to the wall, he fought desperately, until, pierced by English bayonets, he could fight no more. The Bains or Baynes of Tulloch, in Ross-shire, have never used the prefix Mac. The name MacVean is a variation of MacBean.

Chief : MacBain of that Ilk.
Clan Seat : Kinchyle, Inverness-shire.
Tryst : Kinchyle.
Plant : Boxwood.
Memorials : Dunlichity Kirk.

MACBETH

MACBETH or MacBethad MacFinlaeg was a Celtic King of Scotland, whose reign began in 1040, and lasted for seventeen years. He is said to have succeeded his father as ruler of the province of Moray, and married a grand-daughter of Kenneth III. He slew King Duncan, his predecessor. He was himself slain at Lumphanan, Aberdeenshire, in 1057, and was buried in Iona, the common sepulchre for many centuries of the Scottish kings. His step-son Lulach succeeded him, but was slain at Essie in Strathbogie. The race of the Mormairs of Moray for some generations continued unsuccessfully to contest the throne with the line of King Duncan. Their claims were eventually disposed of by a treaty, in which the Lord of the Isles seems to have taken part.

The name was originally a personal one, meaning " lively one." In modern Gaelic it is spelt *Macbheatha*, and another form was *Bethan*. The two names were at a later date merged into the English form of Beaton or Beton. According to the Dean of Lismore, many of the manuscripts in the Advocates' Library were written by the Betons or Macbheaths, who were physicians in Islay and Mull, and also sennachies of the Macleans. The arms recorded are those of George Macbeth.

MACDONALD
THE CLAN DONALD

THE MacDonalds are of very ancient origin. The clan founder was the heroic Somerled, who freed his countrymen from the Norse yoke, and rose to power that no subject has equalled. As Lords of the Isles and Earls of Ross, the Clan Donald were the greatest of the Highland clans, their chief until 1493 ranking as an Island Sovereign. After the fall of the Lords of the Isles, first Glengarry, and then the Lords of Sleat held the chiefship. The branches of Clan Donald were Macalisters, MacIans of Ardnamurchan, Macdonalds of Glencoe, Clanranald, Dunyveg in Islay, Keppoch, Loch Alsh, and Sleat. Glengarry was a cadet of Clanranald. Since 1947 Lord Macdonald has borne the undifferenced arms of the Head of Clan Donald.

Chief : Lord Macdonald.
Patronymic : Mac Dhomnuill.
Clan Seats : Dunscaith Castle ; Armadale Castle ; Ostaig House, all in Skye.
Tryst : DunDonald.
Slogan : Fraoch Eilean.
Plant : Heather.
Memorials : Iona.
Pipe Music : (1) Macdonald's Salute. (2) March of the Macdonalds.

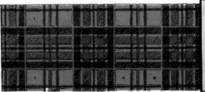

MACDONELL OF KEPPOCH

MACDONALD OF CLANRANALD

THIS clan is derived from Ranald, son of John, 7th Lord of the Isles, by his first wife, Amie MacRuari, who succeeded to Castle Tirrim and the estates of his mother. Dougall, 8th Chief of Clanranald, made himself so hated by cruelty that his clansmen slew him. Command of the clan passed to Alistair, his uncle (to the exclusion of Dougall's son). John of Moydart, his son by a handfast marriage, was "legitimated" in 1531 by the Crown, and invested in the family stronghold as Chief of Clanranald. Ranald, Chief at the time of 1745, was "out" with the Prince —with a following of 700 men.

Chief : Macdonald of Clanranald.

Patronymic : Mac ic' Ailein.

Clan Seat : Ellan Tirrim Castle, Knoydart, Inverness-shire.

Slogan : Dh' aindeòin co theireadh e.

Plant : Heather.

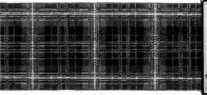

MACDONELL OF GLENGARRY

MACDONALD OF SLEAT

THE house of Macdonald of Sleat, *Clan Huistean*, derives its name and origin from Hugh, a son of Alexander, Lord of the Isles and Earl of Ross, who got Sleat in Skye. Donald Grumach, 4th of Sleat, claimed the Lordship of the Isles but was slain by an arrow at the siege of Ellandonan Castle. In 1680 Sir James Macdonald, 2nd Baronet of Sleat, was recognised in Parliament as Laird of Macdonald, and for Sir Alexander, 7th Baronet, the estate was made a barony of Macdonald—which has devolved to the present Lord Macdonald whilst the chiefship of Clan Huistean has remained with the Baronetcy of Sleat.

Chief : Macdonald of Sleat.
Clan Seat : Duntulm Castle, Skye.
Plant : Heather.

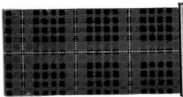

MACDONALD OF ARDNAMURCHAN

MACDOUGALL

THIS is a Celtic clan. The male line of Somerled of the Isles, who died in 1164, is continued in Mac-Dougall of Dunolly, probably descended from Dugall, eldest son of Somerled, ancestor also of the Lords of Lorn. Dugall's grandson was King Ewin of Argyll, 1248. His son was Alexander de Ergadia or Alexander of Argyll. He died 1310, and his son was John of Lorn, Bruce's most obstinate opponent. In the battle of Dalree, 1306, between Bruce and John MacDougall, the famous " Brooch of Lorn " was torn from Bruce's shoulder. It is now owned by MacDougall of Dunolly. Bruce ultimately overcame the clan. Dougall of Dunolly, a direct descendant of MacDougall who opposed Bruce, entered on the lands of Dunolly 1562. Sir John of Dunolly, who succeeded in 1598, married a daughter of Sir Duncan Campbell of Glenorchy. John, styled of Lorn, fought for the Old Chevalier in " the '15," and his lands were forfeited, but afterwards restored and are still held by the present MacDougall of MacDougall. There are MacDougalls of Freugh, Garthland, Gillespick, Logan, Mackerstoun, and Muirtoun. The ancestral burial-place is Ardchattan Priory, on Loch Etive. Several of the clan have been distinguished in war, notably Colonel MacDougall, who, in the Swedish service, defeated the Imperialists at Leignitz.

Chief : MacDougall of MacDougall and Dunollie.
Patronymic : MacDhughaill.
Clan Seats : Dunollie Castle, Oban ; Gylen Castle, Kerrera, Argyll.
Slogan : Buaidh no bas.
Plant : Bell Heather.
Pipe Music : (1) Dunollie Castle. (2) MacDougall's Salute.

MACDUFF

THE first historical mention we have of this clan is of one Dufagan Comes, supposed to be the first of the Celtic Earls of Fife. The Earldom was held " by the Grace of God," and not from the King of Scots, as late as the twelfth century; and a special " Law Clan Macduff " applied there. Constantine, 2nd Earl of Fife in the early years of David's reign died about 1129, and was succeeded by Gillimichel MacDuff, 3rd Earl. The 5th Earl was one of the nobles who treated for the ransom of William the Lion in 1174. His grandson, Malcolm, had two sons— his successor, Colban, and the Macduff who was the primary cause of John Baliol's rebellion against Edward I. The 11th Earl died in 1353, leaving an only daughter, and so the line of the Celtic Earls of Fife ended. It is claimed that David Duff of Muldavit, in Banffshire (1401), was descended from the Earls of Fife. His descendant was William Duff, Lord Braco (1735), who received the titles Viscount Macduff and Earl of Fife in the Peerage of Ireland. The title descended in due course to Alexander, 6th Earl, who was created Duke of Fife in 1889, and that same year married Princess Louise, eldest daughter of King Edward VII. His eldest daughter succeeded as Duchess of Fife in 1912.

Chief : Duff of Braco.
Clan Seats : Duff House, Banff; Keithmore, Dufftown, Banffshire.
Plant : Oak.
Memorials : Duff House Mausoleum.
Pipe Music : The MacDuffs' Gathering.

MACEWAN

COWAL was originally the home of this clan. On the coast of Glenfyne, there stood in 1750 the ruins of MacEwan's Castle. The first MacEwan Chief on record lived in 1200. From this date there were nine chiefs— Swene MacEwen, the 9th, was the last of the Otter Chiefs. In 1431–32 this Swene granted a charter of certain lands of Otter to Duncan, son of Alexander Campbell. This was the beginning of the transference of the MacEwan estates to the Campbells of Argyll. The MacEwans were hereditary bards to the Campbells, for which, we are told, they had free lands. Neil MacEwan composed a Gaelic elegy on Sir Duncan Dow Campbell of Glenorchy in 1630. There is a MS. in Cawdor Castle, entitled " Genealogy Abridgement of the very Ancient and Notable Family of Argyll, 1779," written by MacEwan, hereditary sennachie and bard. The arms shown are those of MacEwan of Glenboy. The chiefship has been claimed by Macewen of Muckley, who has not yet established his right thereto.

MACFARLANE

THIS is a Celtic clan. Their country was the western shore of Loch Lomond. They took their war cry from Loch Sloy, at the foot of Ben Voirlich. They are descended from Duncan MacGilchrist, mentioned 1296, brother of Mulduin, Earl of Lennox. His grandson was Bartholomew (Gaelic, *Parlan*), from whom the clan is named. Malcolm received the lands of Arrochar in 1395, but the male line failed, and the lands were forfeited. Andrew MacFarlane married a daughter of the Earl of Lennox, and succeeded in 1493. Sir John MacFarlane fell at Flodden, and Walter MacFarlane of Tarbert was killed at Pinkie in 1547. The clan fought against Queen Mary at Langside. In 1608 they slew Colquhoun of Luss, and were outlawed. In 1644–45 they fought for Montrose. Major-General MacFarlane gallantly captured Ischia, in the Bay of Naples, in 1809. In 1624 many of the clan settled in Aberdeenshire under other names. The last Chief is supposed to have gone to America at the end of the eighteenth century. His house of Arrochar became the property of the Duke of Argyll, but Macfarlanes of the Kirton line claim the chiefship under a settlement by the last chief of the direct line.

Chief : Macfarlane of that Ilk (*dormant*).

Patronymic : MacPharlain.

Clan Seat : Arrochar.

Slogan : Loch Sloy.

Plant : Cranberry.

Pipe Music : MacFarlane's Gathering, " Lifting the Cattle."

MACFIE

THE Macfies are Celts, and are supposed to be of the race of Alpin. In Gaelic the clan name is *Dubhsithe*— the dark-featured tribe. The English form Duffie has passed into MacDuffie, and further, into Macfie, spelt variously—Macafee, Macfee, and Macphee. In 1549 the island of Colonsay, in Argyll, is recorded to be under the sway of " ane gentle Capitane called Mac-Duffyhe." His descendants, the MacDuffies or Macphees, held the island until the middle of the seventeenth century. Their burial-place was the island Oronsay. The effigies on their tombstones represent them either as warriors or churchmen. In 1645 Coll MacDonald and followers were charged with the murder of Malcolm Macphee of Colonsay. Subsequently the Macphees were dispossessed, and, as a " broken clan," were merged into clans more powerful. Some followed the MacDonalds of Islay; others sheltered under Cameron of Lochiel, and became conspicuous for their courage; while the remainder settled on the shores of Clyde, and even in Ireland, where they were called Macheffie or Macafee. The Macfies, along with the Camerons, charged desperately at Culloden. They were Royalists; and the motto *Pro rege* was recorded as in the arms of Macfie of Dreghorn.

Chief : Macduffie of Colonsay (*dormant*).
Patronymic : Mac-a-Phie.
Clan Seat : Isle of Colonsay.
Plant : Pine.

MACGILLIVRAY

THE MacGillivrays are Celts. They are descended from a warrior named Gillivray, who had his stronghold at Dunmaglass, and who, about the thirteenth century acknowledged himself and his posterity a branch of Clan Chattan under the 5th Mackintosh. The MacGillivrays of Mull and Morven have been said to be a branch of Dunmaglass. In 1579 mention is made of Archibald MacIlvoray in a case between the Laird of Luss and others. The Rev. Martin McGillivray, living in Mull about 1640, carried a claymore, and told Maclaine of Lochbuie that he would use it if he did not pay him his stipend. The MacGillivrays fought for the Old Chevalier at Sheriffmuir in 1715. When Mackintosh refused to lead his clan, which Lady Mackintosh had raised for Prince Charlie, MacGillivray of Dunmaglass took command. He fought like a lion at Culloden, and fell, wounded, in front of Cumberland's 4th Regiment. He was alive next day, and was, by Cumberland's orders, brutally murdered. The Clan Aonghais (Macinnes) formerly wore MacGillivray tartan.

Chief : MacGillivray of Dunmaglass (*dormant*).
Clan Seat : Dunmaglass, Inverness.
Slogan : Dunmaghlas.
Plant : Boxwood.
Memorials : Dunlochity Kirk.
Pipe Music : The MacGillivrays' March.

MACGREGOR

THIS clan claim descent from Gregor, a son of King Alpin, who ruled about 787. They had great possessions in Perthshire and Argyllshire. They held their lands by the sword, fighting bravely for their homes, and gave their enemies such good excuse to urge their dispossession that their name was suppressed by Parliament. In the thirteenth century they held the lands of Glenorchy. Later they appear as tenants of the Campbells. Patrick, who succeeded in 1390, had two younger sons—John Dhu MacGregor of Glenstrae; and Gregor MacGregor of Roro, in Glenlyon. Ultimately the chieftainship went to the Glenstrae branch. In 1502 the line of Roro was dispossessed by the Campbells. In 1603 the MacGregors overthrew their oppressors, the Colquhouns of Luss, at Glenfruin. For this they were outlawed, and their Chief, Alexander MacGregor, with many of his followers, was executed in Edinburgh in 1604; but as late as 1744 MacGregor of Glengyle drew blackmail on the Highland Borders. The suppression of the name was annulled by Parliament in 1774. Rob Roy was of the House of Glengyle. Scott proved that the MacGregors were the real " Children of the Mist." MacGregor of MacGregor and Balquhidder, whose line holds a Baronetcy, has been officially recognised as Chief of the clan.

Chief : MacGregor of MacGregor.
Patronymic : Ant' Ailpeanach.
Clan Seats : Edinchip, Balquhidder; Glenstrae.
Tryst : Ard Coille.
Slogan : Gregalach !
Plant : Scots Fir.
Memorials : Balquhidder Kirk.
Pipe Music : (1) The MacGregors' Gathering. (2) MacGregors' Salute.

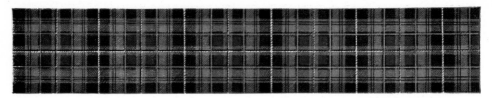

MACINNES

THE name of this clan is *Clan Aonghais* in Gaelic. Its chiefs appear to have been Constables of Kinlochaline Castle. One branch was hereditary bowmen to The Mackinnon.

Patronymic : MacAonghais.
Clan Seat : Kinlochaline Castle, Morvern, Argyll.
Plant : Holly.

MACINTYRE

TRADITIONALLY this clan is a sept of the MacDonalds of Sleat. Glen Noe is given as the original home of the clan. They occupied lands there in the twelfth and thirteenth centuries. These they later held from the Campbells of Glenorchy (afterwards Breadalbane) until 1806. Duncan Macintyre of Glen Noe, first Chief, married Mary, daughter of Patrick Campbell of Barcaldine, by whom he had Donald, his successor. Donald had three children. James, the eldest, succeeded, and was succeeded in turn by his son Donald, a doctor, as 4th Chief of Glen Noe. Duncan, the third son, was a captain in a Highland regiment, and was the last Macintyre of Glen Noe. Dr. Donald emigrated to New York. His son James (5th) and grandson Donald (6th Chief) were well known in the States.

MACKAY

THE clan Mackay derives from a branch of the Royal house of Moray, probably deriving its style *Mac-ic-Morgainn* from Morgund of Pluscarden, a prince of the house of Moray. The first historic Chief was Angus Du (1380–1429). He was assassinated, and the clan was ruled by his younger son, until the rightful heir obtained his release from captivity on the Bass Rock, 1437. The latter's son was Chief and led the clan in the cruel fight of Blair Tannic, Caithness. In 1628 Sir Donald Mackay of Strathnaver, Chief of the clan, was created Lord Reay, with remainder to his heirs-male bearing the name and arms of Mackay.

The major portion of the estates was sold in the seventeenth century to pay the cost of maintaining and transporting 2000 men whom Lord Reay recruited for foreign service to assist the Protestant cause in the great Thirty Years' War. The earliest Gaelic charter extant was granted by Donald, Lord of the Isles, to Brian Vicar Mackay in 1408.

Chief : Lord Reay.
Patronymic : Morair Maghrath.
Clan Seat : House of Tongue, Sutherland.
Slogan : Bratach bhan mhic Aoidh.
Plant : Great Bulrush.
Memorials : Kirk of Tongue.
Pipe Music : (1) Mackay's White Banner. (2) Mackay's March.

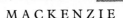

MACKENZIE

THE MacKenzie clan is of Celtic origin. Its home has ever been in Ross-shire; and it rose to power under a great Chief, Alexander *Ionraech*, 7th Chief of Kintail, who ruled in 1427. His grandson, John, 9th Chief, followed James IV to Flodden, and lived to fight for Mary Queen of Scots, at Langside. Kenneth, the next Chief, was in 1609 created Lord Mackenzie of Kintail, and his son Colin, Earl of Seaforth in 1623. William, 5th Earl, was forfeited as a Jacobite in 1715; but his grandson was re-created Earl of Seaforth in 1771, and raised the old Seaforth Highlanders in 1778. His cousin and eventual successor, Francis Humberstone Mackenzie, was re-created Lord Seaforth in 1797; and at his death in 1815 his daughter Mary, Lady Stuart Mackenzie of Seaforth, became *Caberfeidh* and Chief of the clan. Her grandson, James Stewart-Mackenzie, Lord Seaforth of Brahan 1921, was the last chief to hold a peerage, but his heir of line, the Lady of Seaforth, still holds sway in their castle of Brahan. (The sketch represents an officer of the Seaforth Highlanders about 1780.) The chiefship seems at present dormant between three claimants. Mackenzie of Cromartie is nearest heir of line in the "name"; Scatwell is heir-male of Coigeach and so it would appear, of Kintail; but Ord claims to be such heir-male. Gairloch, as oldest cadet, acts as "Commander of the Clan."

Chief : Mackenzie of Kintail.
Patronymic : Caberfeidh.
Clan Seats : Brahan Castle, Urray, Ross-shire; Eilean Donan Castle, Lochalsh.
Slogan : Tulach Ard.
Plant : Deer's Grass
Memorials : Rosemarkie in Ross.
Pipe Music : (1) Mackenzie's Salute. (2) The Mackenzie Highlanders (March).

MACKINLAY

THIS is one of those clans of which we have no very definite account. Lennox is supposed to have been the home of the Mackinlays, and even at the present day they are most numerous around this district. The chief sept of the Mackinlays is stated by some historians as being descended from Finlay Buchanan of Drumikil. At the time of the " Plantations " the Mackinlays, along with other clans, are supposed to have emigrated to Ireland, hence we have the Mackinlays and MacGinlays of that country. From 1527 till 1624 mention is made several times in history of Mackinlays in Dumbarton and Luss. It is singular that no Mackinlay is recorded in all the lists of the 1745 rebels. It is a common mistake to record the clan ancestor as *Fionnlagh Mor*, progenitor of the Farquharsons of Braemar, but the connection is unproved. It is not at all unlikely that the name Mackinlay embraces some of the Macleay clan. There were at one time several *Mac-An-léighs* in Dumbartonshire, and farther north were the *Mac-Onleays*, the real Macleays. The fact that some of the modern Mackinlays insist on accenting the " *ley* " of their name adds weight to this assertion. The Livingstones—another form of Macleay—are the likely forbears of the Mackinlays. Charles Mackinlay of Kynachan in Perthshire got a grant of what appears to be the undifferenced arms of a Mackinlay Chief, and may presumably be regarded as such.

MACKINNON

THIS Celtic clan is mentioned in 1594 as sheltering in the island of Pabay off the coast of Skye, and its chief as owning the Castill of Dunakym and the Castill of Dunningill. In 1409 Lachlan MacFingon, styled gentleman, witnessed a charter by the Lord of the Isles to Maclean of Duart. According to the Lochbuie charter chests, there was an Abbot of Iona named John Mackinnon, who died in 1500. The Mackinnons rebelled with Sir Donald MacDonald of Lochalsh in 1515. In 1545 Ewen, their Chief, was summoned as a rebel. Under Montrose they fought at Inverlochy and Auldearn. In 1650 they fought for Charles II at Worcester. John Dhu Mackinnon of that Ilk and 150 of the clan supported the Chevalier at Sheriffmuir in 1715. John Dhu was attainted, but was pardoned in 1727. The clan was " out " in " the '45." At Culloden their Chief was taken, and was for long imprisoned in the Tower. He died in 1756. The clan has supplied many soldiers of distinction. Strathaird, their last possession, passed from the clan in 1791.

Chief : Mackinnon of Mackinnon.
Patronymic : Mac Fhionghuin.
Clan Seat : Strathardal, in Skye.
Slogan : Cuimhnich bas Ailpein.
Plant : St. John's Wort.
Memorials : Iona.

MACKINTOSH

THIS is a Celtic clan. In 1672 the Chiefs of Mackintosh were declared by the Lord Lyon King of Arms Chiefs of Clan Chattan. There have been Mackintosh Chiefs for nearly five hundred years. Moy is said to have become theirs in 1336. In 1526 Lachlan, Laird of Mackintosh, was slain by James Malcolmson. The Mackintoshes captured Malcolmson, and cut him to pieces. In 1550 William, 15th Mackintosh, paid a friendly visit to Huntly Castle, but was treacherously beheaded by order of the Countess. In 1689 Mackintosh claimed Glenroy and Glenspean. Keppoch kept him out, and defeated him at Mulroy, the last clan battle. Mackintosh died 1704. His son, Lachlan, died childless, 1731, and for a hundred years thereafter no son succeeded a father amongst the Mackintosh chiefs, this remarkable occurrence being ascribed to the curse said to have been placed on the Chief by a jilted lady. The clan fought at Culloden. The Chief remained neutral, and MacGillivray of Dunmaglass commanded. Æneas Mackintosh of Mackintosh was created a Baronet by George III, but died childless. His kinsman, the Hon. Angus Mackintosh, residing in Canada, succeeded him, and from him descended the subsequent chiefs. The Mackintosh country is Brae Lochaber, Badenoch, and Strathnairn. The clan historian described the chiefship of the Mackintoshes as territorial—passing with the *duthus*, where their home, Moy Hall, stands on the shore of Loch Moigh.

Chief : Mackintosh of Mackintosh.
Patronymic : Mac-an-Toisich.
Clan Seats : Moy Hall, Inverness ; Dunauchton.
Tryst : Loch Moy.
Slogan : Loch Moigh.
Plant : Red Whortleberry/Bearberry.
Memorials : Kirk of Petty, Moray.
Pipe Music : The Mackintosh's Banner (Salute).

MACLACHLAN

MACLACHLAN is a Celtic clan. The MacLachlans of that Ilk have resided from time immemorial in Strathlachlan, in Argyllshire. The district was once called Kilmorlie. The first authentic record is that the lands of Gileskel MacLachlan were included in the Sheriffdom of Argyll or Lorn in 1292 by King John Baliol and a charter granted him, and his name appears on the Roll of Magnates of Scotland who sat in the first Parliament of Robert the Bruce at St. Andrews. The name Lachlanson occurs in three charters by Robert the Bruce. In 1587 and 1594 Archibald MacLachlan of Strathlachlan and that Ilk is mentioned. " Corronel MacLachlan " was captured at Philiphaugh in 1645, and executed in Edinburgh Castle. Lachlan MacLachlan, Chief of the clan, was A.D.C. to Prince Charlie. He was killed at Culloden. It is said that his horse made its way home to Strathlachlan alone after the battle. In 1794 Donald MacLachlan of that Ilk was Chief; and the ancient castle has continued to descend to successive chiefs of the clan. There are MacLachlans in Morvern and Lochaber, the principal family of which is Mac-Lachlan of Coruanan.

Chief : MacLachlan of MacLachlan.
Clan Seat : Castle-Lachlan, Strathlachlan, Argyll.
Plant : Rowan.
Pipe Music : Moladh Mairi (Salute).

MACLAINE OF LOCHBUIE

THE Maclaines of Lochbuie are Celtic. Their remote ancestor was Hector Reaganach, brother of Lachlan Lùbanach, ancestor of the Meacleans of Duart, who were the offspring of Black John of Mull. Some say that Hector Reaganach was the elder brother ; but in any case the chiefship was settled on Duart by Tanistry, so that Lochbuie is a branch-clan under the " Lairds of Maclean." Hector persuaded a neighbouring Chief, MacFadyean, to let him build a castle on a high rock above the sea, and then used the advantage thus given him to add the lands of this Chief to his own. A Chief of Lochbuie died and left an infant son ; Maclean of Duart annexed the lands of his young kinsman, who was saved by being sent to Ireland. Maclaine, on reaching manhood, returned and recovered his castle and estates. On one occasion Lochbuie came upon Duart sleeping after battle, in which he had defeated him. He twisted his dirk in Duart's hair and stuck in the ground. Duart, on waking, knew the dirk, and made friends with Lochbuie. The Maclaines fought gallantly for Claverhouse and for Montrose. The famous Sir Archibald Maclaine, K.T., C.B., was a cadet of the House of Lochbuie. Maclaine of Lochbuie is the present representative ; but the estate was seized by an English creditor.

Chief : Maclaine of Lochbuie.
Patronymic : Mac-ill-Eathain Lochabuidhe.
Clan Seat : Lochbuie Castle, Mull, Argyll.
Plant : Bilberry/Bramble.

MACLAREN

THIS is an ancient clan, an early branch, it is believed of the early dynasts of Strathearn. Their chiefs were Hereditary Celtic Abbots of Achtow, in Perthshire, and of the many origins the most probable is that they are descended from Abbot Lawrence. Their country lay between Lochearnhead and Glengyle, and they appear in the Ragman Roll of 1296. They were allies of the Stewarts of Appin through a love-at-first-sight episode, and their feuds were frequent with the Buchanans, Campbells, and MacGregors. They fought at Bannockburn, at Flodden, and at Pinkie. They have been distinguished in peace. The Psalms were translated into Gaelic by Colin MacLaren or MacLaurin, son of the Rev. John MacLaurin, minister of Glendaruel. Colin was born at Kilmodan in 1698. He was Professor of Mathematics in Edinburgh University in 1745. For having planned the defence of the city against Prince Charlie he had to abscond to York. The clan fought for Prince Charlie at Culloden. The clan burial-place is Leackine, by Loch Earn. The house of MacLaren of Auchleskine came to be chiefs and the heir of this line was by Lyon Court adjudged to be Maclaren of Maclaren in 1957.

Chief : MacLaren of MacLaren.
Patronymic : Mac-aub's Labhran.
Clan Seats : Auchleskine and Achtow in Balquhidder, Perthshire.
Tryst : Creag-an-tuirc, Balquhidder.
Sloan : Creag-an-Tuirc.
Plant : Laurel.
Memorials : Balquhidder Kirk.

MACLEAN OF DUART

DUART CASTLE
MULL.

THE Macleans of Duart are Celtic. They claim descent from a famous Celtic warrior, Gillean of the Battle Axe, and have lived in Mull from a very remote time. They were vassals of the Lords of the Isles, but became independent on the forfeiture of the latter in 1476. In many old deeds and Acts of Parliament their chief is styled "Laird of Maclean." Duart Castle, facing Lismore, is their family stronghold. Their Chief, Hector, was slain at Flodden. Lachlan Cattanach Maclean of Duart left his wife on a low rock, hoping that the returning tide would drown her, but she was rescued, and her husband was assassinated in Edinburgh by her brother, Sir John Campbell. Another Lachlan harried the other Macleans and the MacDonalds. He fell in battle with the MacDonalds of Islay in 1598. Sir John Maclean fought with Claverhouse at Killiecrankie and with Mar at Sheriffmuir. The clan was in the front line at Culloden under the Duke of Perth. On the death of Sir Hector Maclean in 1750 the title passed to his cousin, great-grandson of Maclean of Brolass, from whom descended the centenarian Chief, Colonel Fitzroy Donald Maclean of Duart and Morvern, Bart., who restored the ancestral castle of Duart in Mull.

Chief : Maclean of Duart.
Patronymic : Mac-ill-Eathain.
Clan Seat : Duart Castle, Mull.
Slogan : Fear-eile-airson-Eachuinn.
Plant : Crowberry.

MACLENNAN OR LOGAN

THIS clan's origin is Celtic. Tradition says that at Drumderfit, where the Frasers defeated the Logans, a warrior called Gilligorm was slain. His posthumous son was born among the Frasers, who intentionally broke the child's back. The boy was called Crotair MacGilligorm. He became a priest, and founded a church at Kilmuir, in Skye, and another at Glenelg. He flourished in the thirteenth century. As Celtic Church priests were allowed to marry, he had a son called Gille Fhinnein, from whom the Maclennans are descended. The Maclennans were numerous in Kintail. At Auldearn in 1645 Lord Seaforth, opposing Montrose, intended to change sides. The clansmen, unaware of this, refused to retreat when ordered to do so. Maclennan, the standard-bearer, planted the standard and defended it until he was shot down. There are still Maclennans in the neighbourhood of Brahan, the castle built by Colin, 1st Earl of Seaforth, in the seventeenth century. John Ferguson Maclennan (1827–1881), author of *Primitive Marriage*, was a member of the clan. The Maclennan Chiefs are said to have been Bannermen to Mackenzie of Kintail (Seaforth). The arms shown are those of Logan of that Ilk.

Chief : (*Logan*) Logan of Drumderfit.
Patronymic : Ghillinnein.
Clan Seat : Drumderfit, Ross-shire (Black Isle).
Tryst : Druic-na-Claven, Kintail.
Slogan : Druim-nan deur.
Plant : Furze.

DUNVEGAN CASTLE
SKYE

MACLEOD OF MACLEOD

THE MacLeods are Norse, and are descended from Tormod, son of Leod, who was the son of Olave the Black, King of Man. They were vassals of the Lords of the Isles, but became independent when that Lordship was forfeited. The Harris Chief is variously styled "MacLeod of MacLeod, MacLeod of that Ilk and of Harris." Tormod received Glenelg from David II (Charter, 1344). His descendants held Harris, St. Kilda, and vast estates in Skye. In 1577 MacLeod of Dunvegan suffocated the entire population of Eigg in a cave. Rory More, outlaw, then trusted Royal servant (1595–1626) and Ian Breac (seventeenth century), a model Chief, were MacLeods of Dunvegan. Of Dunvegan also was General MacLeod of MacLeod, who raised the second battalion of the 42nd. Dunvegan Castle is still the abode of the MacLeods of that Ilk. The 27th Chief, Sir Reginald MacLeod of MacLeod, K.C.B., died in 1935, and was succeeded by his daughter, Dame Flora MacLeod of MacLeod, 28th chief of the clan.

Chief : MacLeod of MacLeod.
Patronymic : MacLeoid.
Clan Seat : Dunvegan Castle, Isle of Skye.
Plant : Juniper.
Memorials : Rodill, in Harris.
Pipe Music : MacLeod's Salute ; MacLeod's Rowing Salute.

MACLEOD OF LEWIS

THE MacLeods of Lewis (like the MacLeods of MacLeod) are of Norse origin, and were owners of the Lewis and of Waternish in Skye. They had also Assynt on the mainland by Crown charter, 1340. Along with the clansmen of the Harris branch they fought on the right wing at Harlaw in 1411. At the close of the sixteenth century the male line of the MacLeod of Lewis became extinct. The lands of Assynt passed to the Earl of Seaforth in 1660. The story of how this came about is one of the darkest and bloodiest pages in the troubled history of the Highland clans. Their estates were transferred to MacKenzie of Kintail, and MacLeod of Raasay claimed to have become heir-male, but was not allowed arms as representor. Raasay also lost his lands, but continued to be principal cadet of *Siol Torquil*. The MacLeods fought for Charles II at Worcester, but took no active part in future Jacobite risings. The tartans shown above first appeared as the dress tartans of MacLeod of MacLeod.

Clan Seats : Stornoway Castle (ruined fragment), Lewis ; Assynt, Ross-shire.
Plant : Red Whortleberry.

MACMILLAN

THE Macmillans are Celts, but whether their first location was in Argyll, Breadalbane, or Lochaber, is a matter of dispute. It is certain they had possessions on both sides of Loch Arkaig. A branch of them appeared in Knapdale, Argyllshire, in the sixteenth century. Their feudal grant of Knap from the Lord of the Isles was destined to Macmillan " so long as the wave beats on the rock." By marriage, one of their chieftains became allied to the MacNeills, and owned Castle Sweyn. The Chief of the Knapdale branch was called Macmillan of Knap. These Macmillans built the Chapel of Kilmore. In their burial-place there is a high stone cross with the legend in Latin : " This is the cross of Alexander Macmillan." The Macmillans of Glen Shera, Glen Shira, and others, are descended from a clansman, Gille Maol, who settled at Badokenan on Loch Fyne. The Knapdale succession became extinct, and Macmillan of Dunmore was made Chief. His line also became extinct, and both the Campbells and the MacNeills claimed the lands. The Campbells got possession. The Macmillans of Lochaber were faithful followers of Lochiel. A branch of the clan also settled in Galloway. In later times others went to Arran. The estates were purchased in 1775 by Sir Archibald Campbell of Inverneil. The tartan illustrated is that termed " Macmillan, Ancient." In 1951 Lieut.-Gen. Sir Gordon Macmillan of Macmillan and Knap was revested as Chief of the Clan.

Chief : Macmillan of Macmillan.
Patronymic : Mac-Mhaoilean-mor-a-Cnaip.
Clan Seat : Knapdale.
Tryst : Macmillan's Cross, Knapdale.
Plant : Holly.
Memorials : Resby-Cnaip.

MACNAB

THE ancestor of this Celtic clan was the Abbot of the monastery of St. Fillan in Glendochart. The office of Abbot became secularised and hereditary in one family. The Macnabs lost nearly all their lands through joining with the MacDougalls against Bruce. In the reign of James IV a decisive battle was fought between them and their deadly enemies, the Neishes; the Macnabs won. The Neishes sheltered on the island in Loch Earn. In James V's reign, " Smooth John Macnab " and his twelve sons stole upon the Neishes and slew them all " save one and a boy." In 1646 the Macnabs defended the Castle of Kincardine, cut their way through Sir John Middleton's Guards, and fought for Montrose. John Macnab of that Ilk fell at Worcester. In 1654 the Laird of Glenorchy assisted " in putting the haill Maknabs out of the country." The Chief's family fought for the House of Hanover in " the '45," but the clan fought for the Stewarts. The 12th Chief is the subject of Raeburn's great portrait, " The Macnab." Archibald, the 13th Chief, sold his estates, and with some hundreds of the clan, emigrated to Canada. He died in France in 1860. His daughter, Sophia Frances, died in 1894. There are Macnabs of Acharn, Inchewen, Dundurn, Strathfillan, Suie, Newton, Cowie, Jamaica, and others.

Chief : Macnab of Macnab.
Patronymic : Mac-an-Aba.
Clan Seats : Kinnell, Killin, Perthshire ; Bovain, Perthshire.
Slogan : Bovain.
Plant : Stone Bramble.
Memorials : Innis Buie.
Pipe Music : Macnab's Gathering.

84

MACNAUGHTEN

THE MacNaughtens are of Celtic origin. They are descended from a Pictish king named Nechtan or Nauchten, who founded Abair Neachtain or Abernethy. Their lands lay along the shore of Loch Awe, in Lorn. Alexander III granted the custody of the castle and island of Fraoch Eilean, in Loch Awe, to Gilchrist MacNaughten. The clan fought against Bruce. In 1426 Donald MacNaughten was Bishop-elect of Dunkeld. Sir Alexander MacNaughten of that Ilk was slain at Flodden. Alexander MacNaughten of that Ilk raised a magnificent band of Archers for Charles I. whom he served faithfully. He clove to Charles II likewise, was a courtier, and died in London. A complimentary letter was sent by James VII to Mac-Naughten of that Ilk in 1689. A branch of the clan settled in Antrim, Ireland. They acquired an estate and castle called Benuardin and were honoured with a Baronetcy. Their line was recognised as chiefs by the Court of the Lord Lyon, and the present Baronet is the Chief of Clan MacNaughten. The old seat of the race was Dunderawe Castle, a tall tower on Loch Fyne.

Chief : MacNaughten of Dunderawe.
Clan Seat : Dunderawe (Castle of the Two Oars), Argyll.
Slogan : Frechelan.
Plant : Trailing Azalea.

85

KISMUL CASTLE
BARRA.

MACNEIL OF BARRA

THE MacNeils of Barra and the McNeills of Gigha are Celtic, and according to some sennachies trace their common origin to Neil Og. Neil, the founder of the clan, lived about 1300. The earliest mention of a charter to a MacNeil of Barra—named Gilleonan—is of date 1427. Gilleonan, the 9th of Barra, is on record in 1545. The Chapel of St. Barr was the burial-place of the MacNeils of Barra. In 1587 Queen Elizabeth complained that Roderick MacNeil of Barra had seized an English ship. Roderick did not appear at Edinburgh when summoned, but he was captured by MacKenzie of Kintail, and conveyed to Edinburgh. Barra was forfeited and given to Kintail. The superiority of Barra passed to Sir James MacDonald of Sleat until 1688. In 1650 MacNeil of Barra was among the "Scottish Colonells of Horsse." In 1688 Roderick MacNeil, 14th of Barra, obtained a Crown charter of Barra, making it a free barony. Several MacNeils named Roderick succeeded. In 1840 Barra was sold to Colonel John Gordon of Cluny. The 25th Chief, Robert Lister MacNeil of Barra, recovered the island of Barra and Kismull Castle, the island fortress and home of the chiefs.

Chief : The MacNeil of Barra.
Patronymic : MacNeill.
Clan Seat : Kismull Castle, Isle of Barra.
Slogan : Buaidh-no-Bas.
Plant : Seaware.

McNEILL OF GIGHA

SO far back as 1472 the McNeills of Gigha were Keepers of the Castle of Sweyn, in North Knapdale, Argyllshire. The Lord of the Isles was their overlord. Neil McNeill was Chief of the clan or branch-clan in the first half of the sixteenth century. He had a son, Neil, from whom the McNeills of Taynish are descended. Another son, John Og, was the ancestor of the McNeills of Gallachoille and of Crerar, afterwards of Colonsay. James MacDonald of Islay purchased Gigha in 1554. It was acquired later by John Campbell of Calder, who sold it in 1590 to Hector McNeill of Taynish. Gigha and Taynish were owned by his descendants till 1780. In that year Alexander McNeill of Colonsay purchased Gigha. In addition to the Taynish family, there were McNeills of Gallachoille, Caraskey, Tir Fergus. In the seventeenth century Torquil, of the House of Tir Fergus, married the heiress of the Mackays, and acquired the lands of Ugadale, in Kintyre. The present owner is called MacNeal. Sir John McNeill, K.C.B., LL.D., Envoy at the Court of Persia, 1831, belonged to the Colonsay branch. Hector McNeill, who wrote " Come under my Plaidie," was a member of the Clan McNeill. He died at Edinburgh in 1818. The children of the house of McNeill were, according to old Highland custom, taught their genealogy in Gaelic on Sunday morning.

Clan Seats : Isles of Gigha and Colonsay ; Castle-Sweyn, Knapdale.
Plant : Dryas.

MACNICOL OR NICOLSON

THE origin of this clan is difficult to determine, but Skye seems to be their native place. The Nicolsons held the lands of Scorrybreck, Skye, from about the middle of the eleventh century. A history of the MacDonalds, written in the reign of Charles II, makes mention of MacNicol of Portree. In 1263, at the battle of Largs, Sir Andrew Nicolson, a Danish knight from the Isle of Skye, commanded one of Haco's ships. Members of the family settled at Lonfeaon, Penefiler Aird, and elsewhere in Skye, but Nicolson of Scorrybreck was always looked upon as the head of the clan in the west. Norman Nicolson of Scorrybreck emigrated to New Zealand, and his descendants still subsist there. The arms of the Chief—representative of Scorrybreck—are duly recorded in Lyon Register. The late Alexander Nicolson, LL.D., advocate, distinguished himself in the Celtic field. Born at Hugobost, Skye, in 1827, called to the Bar in 1860, he was commissioned to report upon the state of education in the Highlands in 1865. He was also a member of Lord Napier's Commission appointed in 1883 to inquire into the condition of the crofters.

Chief : Nicolson of Scorrybreac.
Patronymic : M'Nicaill.
Clan Seat : Scorrybreac House, Skye.
Slogan : Scorr-A-Bhreac.
Memorials : Snizort, in Skye.

MACPHERSON

THE Macphersons are Celts. The Chief is called Cluny Macpherson. The Macphersons of Invereshie (now Macpherson Grants of Ballindalloch) are another branch. This branch is called *Sliochd Gillies*. Skene traces the Cluny family from Duncan, the Parson, 1438. Duncan was from Strathnairn. The Invereshie Macphersons are from Badenoch. Andrew Macpherson in Cluny and of Grange, in Banffshire, was tenant in Cluny in 1603. Duncan Macpherson of Cluny was in 1672 defeated by Mackintosh in obtaining official recognition as Chief of Clan Chattan. The Invereshie and Pitmean families opposed, being real Badenoch Macphersons descended from Muireach Parson. Duncan died in 1722. The Macphersons had now been recognised by Lyon Court as a clan, and Cluny as Chief given " supporters." Lachlan Macpherson married a daughter of Lochiel. He died in 1746. His son, Ewen, who married Lord Lovat's daughter, fought for Prince Charlie. In 1784 the estates were restored to his son, Duncan, whose son, Ewen, the next Chief, died in 1885. Duncan Macpherson of this clan led the Black Watch over the trenches of Tel-el-Kebir. Their Chief's seat was long at Cluny Castle, Kingussie, Inverness-shire ; but this has been sold, and the present Cluny Macpherson is in Australia.

Chief : Macpherson of Cluny (*Cluny Macpherson*).
Patronymic : MacMhuirich.
Clan Seat : Cluny-in-Badenoch, Kingussie.
Tryst : Lochan Ovie, Creag Dhu.
Slogan : Creag-dhubh.
Plant : White heather.
Pipe Music : Cluny-Macpherson's Salute ; Macpherson's March.

MACQUARRIE

THE Clan Macquarrie is Celtic. They first appeared in possession of the island of Ulva and part of Mull. John Macquarrie of Ulva died about 1473, and is the first prominently mentioned. After the forfeiture of the Lord of the Isles they followed the Macleans of Duart. In 1504 MacGorry of Ullowaa was summoned for rebelling with Donald Dubh, who claimed the Lordship of the Isles. In 1609 Andrew Knox, Bishop of the Isles, received as King's Commissioner at Iona the submission of Ulva and other Chiefs. In 1778 Lachlan Macquarrie of Ulva sold his property and became a soldier at the age of sixty-three. When the old 74th Regiment, Argyll Highlanders, was raised, Lachlan Macquarrie became one of the officers. The direct line of the Macquarries of Ulva became extinct in 1818. Later scions have been traced in India and Lauchlan Macquarries, Governor of New South Wales, 1809–21, was a cousin of the then Chief.

Chief : Macquarrie of Ulva (*dormant*).
Patronymic : Mac-Cuaire.
Clan Seat : Isle of Ulva.
Slogan : An t-arm-breac-dearg.
Plant : Pine.
Pipe Music : The Red-Tartaned Army.

MACQUEEN

THE Macqueens or Clan Revan are a Celtic race. They were of the Hebrides, and the founder of the clan is supposed to have been Roderick Dhu Revan MacSweyn or Macqueen. In the thirteenth century Castle Sween, in Kintyre, was occupied by MacSweens. There were MacSweens among the Lamont clansmen executed at Dunoon in 1646. The ancestor of the MacEwans was called Swene MacEwan. The Hebridean Macqueens were subject to the Lords of the Isles. The Macqueens of Corrybrough, an offshoot, settled in Strathdearn. When the 10th Mackintosh married Mora MacDonald of Moidart, Revan-MacMulmor MacAngus and Donald MacGillandrish came with the bride, and settled near her new abode.

John and Sweyn Macqueen signed the Clan Chattan Bond of 1609. Captain Donald Macqueen, 7th of Corrybrough, died in 1813. He was succeeded by his son, Donald, Captain 2nd Madras Cavalry, who was succeeded by his brother, John Fraser Macqueen, Q.C. He died in 1881. The chiefship, but not the estate, fell to his brother, Lachlan, of the East India Company. Lachlan died in 1896, and was succeeded by his only son, Donald, as Chief, who was resident in New Zealand. The Macqueens of Pollochaig, Clune and Strathnoon are the leading cadets. The Clan MacSweyn is officially regarded as distinct from that of Macqueen, and the arms of the MacSweyn Chief have been registered as such.

Clan Seats : Corrybrough, Strathdearn, Inverness-shire.
Plant : Red Whortleberry.
Pipe Music : Lament for MacSween of Roaig.

MACRAE

THIS clan is Celtic. Macrae in Gaelic is *MacRath*, and means " Son of Grace." The home of the " Wild Macraes " was Kintail, where they did great service for the Earls of Seaforth. They were Constables of Eilean Donan Castle. The Rev. Farquhar Macrae (1580–1662), Vicar of Kintail, was a man of mark, Sir John Macrae (1786–1847) of Ardintoul, an eminent soldier, and Rev. John Macrae (1794–1876) of Knockbain, a famous divine. As Jacobites, Macraes fought at Sheriffmuir, 1715, and loyally afterwards for the House of Hanover. In 1778 the Macraes were ringleaders in the mutiny of the Seaforth Highlanders in Edinburgh, when entrenched on Arthur's Seat, refusing to yield until peacefully approached, and their terms of enlistment fulfilled. Brig.-Gen. William Macrae (1834–82) was distinguished in the American Confederate army. Maj. Robert M'Crea, of Guernsey (1754–1835), was a loyalist in the American War of Independence. The late Constable of Eilean Donan Castle, Macrae-Gilstrap of Ballimore, restored the picturesque fortress at Lochalsh. The house of Inverinate appears to have been always the principal stock of the clan.

Patronymic : MacRath.
Clan Seat : Inverinate, Inverness-shire.
Slogan : Sgùr Urain.
Plant : Club Moss.
Memorials : Kintail, Auld Kirk.
Pipe Music : The Macraes' March.

MACTAVISH

MACTAVISH is the modern spelling of this clan's name. Originally it had many forms, chief of which were Thompson, Thomason, MacOmish and MacCombie derived from MacTommie, and Mac-Thamais or MacTavish, from the Scots Tammas. In Perthshire, as early as 1488, Donald MacCause (another form of the name) obtained lands near Killin, where he died in 1491. Many of the Argyllshire MacTavishes have changed their name to Thompson. This family claim to be a sept of the Clan Campbell, descended from a son of Colin, the third Campbell, from whom are descended Clan Tavish Campbell. MacTavish of Dunardy was Chief of the clan, and the heir of this line is understood to be now in Canada but has not yet lodged a claim to the arms and chiefship.

Chief : MacTavish of MacTavish.
Clan Seat : Dunardy, Argyll.

MALCOLM OR MACCALLUM

HISTORY is rather confusing as to the correct origin of this clan. Tradition has it that the family settled at an early period in Argyllshire, yet in the reigns of David II and Robert II we find charters granting lands to Malcolms in Stirlingshire. Their territory lay in the Loch Awe district, and they are traditionally reported to be an offshoot of the MacGhille Challums (or MacLeods) of Raasay. They took protection of the Campbells of Lochow, and in 1414 Sir Duncan Campbell of Lochow granted to Reginald MacCallum of Corbarron certain lands, together with the office of Hereditary Constable of the Castles of Lochaffy and Craignish, but this branch appears to have become extinct during the latter half of the seventeenth century. Dugald MacCallum of Poltalloch inherited the estate in 1779, and was the first to adopt the name of Malcolm permanently. Admiral Sir Pulteney Malcolm was Commander-in-Chief of St. Helena, and won the regard of Napoleon. John Wingfield Malcolm of Poltalloch was created Lord Malcolm in 1896, and died in 1902, when the peerage became extinct, though his brother inherited his estate, and the feudal title of " Malcolm of Poltalloch " descended with the chiefship of the clan. The tartan shown has been approved as correct by Sir Ian Malcolm of Poltalloch.

Chief : Malcolm of Poltalloch.
Clan Seat : Poltalloch, Argyll.
Plant : Rowan Berries.

MATHESON

THE clan was called in Gaelic *Mac-mthathan* or *Mac-mhaghan*. Their first appearance in history is in 1262–63 when Kermac Macmaghan assisted the Earl of Ross against the Norse. The pedigree MS. of 1467 gives the Chiefs from 1263 to 1400, thus: " Mathan, father of Kenneth, father of Murdoch, father of Duncan, father of Murdoch, father of Murdoch." The latter was probably Makmaken of Bower, the Chief in 1427. John du Matheson, Constable of Ellandonan Castle, was father of Dugall Roy, and grandfather of Murdoch Buidhe, a notable personage in 1570–90. All the Matheson genealogies of the present day converge on Murdoch Buidhe. This Murdoch Buidhe had two sons : Roderick of Fernaig, and Dugall of Balmacara, Chamberlain of Lochalsh. The descendants of the former were proprietors of the estate of Bennetsfield, in the Black Isle. In 1899 the representation of the family of Bennetsfield devolved upon Heylin Fraser Matheson, grandson of Charles Mac-Kenzie Matheson, third son of Colin of Bennetsfield. Other important branches of the clan are the Mathesons of Shinness, in Sutherland, and of Achany. The line of Matheson of Attadale, dating from about 1730 (and descending from Dougall of Balmacara), acquired a Baronetcy in 1882.

Slogan : Acha-'n-da-thearnaid.
Plant : Broom.

MAXWELL

THE first mention we have of the Maxwell clan is Sir John Maxwell, Chamberlain of Scotland, who died without issue in 1241. He was succeeded by his brother, who, with other children, had two sons, Herbert and John. Sir Herbert's descendant in the seventh degree was created Lord Maxwell, and had two sons— Robert, 2nd Lord, and Sir Edward. From the latter come the Maxwells of Monreith. Robert, 2nd Lord Maxwell, was succeeded by his son John, who fell at Flodden, 1513, when the title went to his son. The latter had two sons—Robert, 5th Lord, and Sir John, who became Lord Herries of Terregles. Robert, 5th Lord, was succeeded by his son, 6th Lord, who in turn was succeeded by his son John; the latter was executed for murder, and the title fell to his brother, Robert, afterwards Earl of Nithsdale. His son, Robert, dying without issue, the estates reverted to his cousin, Lord Herries, whose son and grandson held the Earldom in turn. The latter was sentenced to death as a Jacobite, but, by the aid of his wife, escaped to Rome, where he died in 1744. He left a son, William, whose great-grandson proved his claim to the Barony of Herries. He died in 1876, succeeded by his son, Marmaduke (Lord Herries). Sir John Maxwell of Pollok, great-grandson of Sir Aymer, second son of Sir Aymer, had two sons, Sir John and Sir Robert. From the latter come the Maxwells of Cardoness, also those of Farnham. From the former come the Maxwells of Pollok, Baronets. The great Border castle of Caerlaverock was long the seat of the Maxwell Chiefs.

Clan Seat : Caerlaverock Castle, Dumfriesshire.
Plant : Rowan.

MENZIES

THE ancient home of this clan has ever been Castle-Menzies at Weem in Perthshire. The three-davoch land of Weem was, in the reign of Alexander III, confirmed by John, Earl of Atholl, to Sir Alexander, son and heir of Sir Robert de Meyners. His descendant, Sir Robert de Menzies, 1479–1523, got Weem erected into a Barony by James III; and in 1510 James IV ordained the house to be named Castle-Menzies. It was reconstructed by James Menzies of that Ilk, 1571. Sir Alexander Menzies of that Ilk was created Baronet, 1665. In 1746 Sir Robert, 3rd Baronet, entertained Prince Charlie at Castle-Menzies, his kinsman, Colonel Ian Menzies of Shian, having raised a regiment for the Prince. Sir Neil, 6th Baronet of that Ilk, raised the clan to welcome Queen Victoria at Loch Tay in 1842; and in 1894 under Sir Robert, 7th Baronet, the Clan Menzies Society was established. The Baronetcy expired with Sir Neil, 8th Baronet, in 1910; and on the death of his sister, Miss Menzies of Menzies, the chiefship passed to Steuart-Menzies of Culdares and Arndilly, who has since re-acquired Castle-Menzies and has been confirmed in the style *Menzies of that Ilk* (The Menzies).

Chief : Menzies of that Ilk.
Patronymic : Am-Meinnearach (*The Menzies*).
Clan Seat : Castle-Menzies, Weem, Aberfeldy.
Tryst : The Rock of Weem.
Slogan : Geal is Dearg a Suas.
Plant : Menzies Heath.
Memorials : Auld Kirk o' Weem.
Pipe Music : The Menzies' Salute ; Menzies' March.

MORRISON

THE Morrisons claim to be of Scandinavian extraction, and their original home was Lewis and the north-west of Scotland. The first Morrison of importance, according to history, Hugh or Hucheon, the Brieve, held the office of Hereditary Deemster or judge in Lewis and adjacent islands, in which office he was succeeded by his son John. The Morrisons at this time had many feuds with the MacLeods, the former having to take refuge with their kinsmen in Durness and Edderachyllis. Apparently juridical duties were unpleasant in the Hebrides. It was only when the MacKenzies acquired Lewis in 1610 that the Morrisons had peace. From that period they were chiefly known as churchmen, several of them being prominent ministers. The Rev. Kenneth Morrison of Lewis was an ancestor of Lord Macaulay through his daughter Margaret having married Rev. Aulay Macaulay, great-grandfather of Lord Macaulay. John Morrison of Bragar, grandson of Brieve John, was a famous wit and poet. The Harris branch of the family produced a succession of noted armourers and smiths. Donald Morrison of Skinidin, Skye, married a daughter of John Breac MacLeod of MacLeod. The most noted of this family was Captain Alexander Morrison, who assisted " Ossian Macpherson." Morrisons are still an important clan in the Hebrides and the north-west of Scotland. The Morrisons of Ruchdi are descended from the Herrach'd-fhear of Pabbay-of-Tarbert in Harris, and from them came Viscount Dunrossil, whilst the " landed men " of the clan are submitting a proposed chief to the Lord Lyon for confirmation, and Duneystein has been re-acquired for his seat.

Chief : Morrison of Barvas and Duneystein.

Patronymic : Mac Gulle-Mhoire.

Clan Seats : Duneystein Castle, Isle of Lewis ; Dun of Pabbay-of-Tarbert in Harris.

Tryst : Duneystein.

Slogan : Duneystein.

Plant : Driftwood.

MUNRO

MUNRO of Foulis has always been the title of the Chief of Clan Munro. The first assured Chief by Charter is Robert de Munro (1341–72). Robert Munro (16th) was succeeded by his brother, Hector, who had two sons and a daughter. The eldest, Sir Robert, his successor, called the Black Baron, was Colonel of two Dutch regiments. He died, leaving no male issue, so the estate devolved upon his brother, Hector, who was created a Baronet of Nova Scotia in 1634. He married Mary, daughter of Hugh Mackay of Farre. On his death he was succeeded by his only son, Sir Hector, who died without issue, so the title went to his cousin, Robert, 3rd Baronet. He married his cousin (a sister of Sir Hector), by whom he had seven sons. The eldest and his son held the title in turn, the latter being appointed High Sheriff of Ross in 1725. Among the distinguished members of this clan were those who shed lustre on the School of Anatomy in Edinburgh—Alexander the first, Alexander the second, and Alexander the third, son of the second. There was also Donald Munro, M.D., an eminent medical writer. We must also mention Sir Hector Munro, K.C.B., Colonel of the Black Watch, who died at Novar, Ross-shire, in 1805. On the death of Sir Hector Munro of Foulis, 11th Baronet, the *duthus* and chiefship passed to his daughter, and were in due course passed on to her son as Laird of Foulis and Chief of Clan Munro.

Chief : Munro of Foulis.
Patronymic : Tighearna-Folais.
Clan Seat : Foulis Castle, Evanton, Ross-shire.
Tryst : Foulis Castle.
Slogan : Caisteal Fòlais na Theine.
Plant : Common Club Moss.
Pipe Music : Munros' Salute ; Munros' March.

99

BLAIR CASTLE
PERTHSHIRE

MURRAY OF ATHOLL

FRESKIN, ancestor of the great family of Murray, was, there is reason to believe, a Pictish noble of the old race of Moray. His grandson, William, assumed the name " De Moravia." From him is decended the great house of which Lyon Court has judicially held is now the chiefly line of the Murrays. Sir John Murray, 12th feudal Baron of Tullibardine, was by James VI in 1606 created Earl of Tullibardine, Lord Murray, Gask and Balquhidder. William, 2nd Earl of Tullibardine, married Lady Dorothea Stewart, daughter and heir-in-line of the 5th Earl of Atholl, who died 1594. His son John, as heir-of-line of the Stewart Earls of Atholl, was in 1629 by King Charles I confirmed in his mother's peerage, and so became the 1st Murray Earl of Atholl. John, 2nd Earl, was created Marquis of Atholl, 1676, and John, 2nd Marquis, Duke of Atholl in 1703. His eldest son, William, Marquis of Tullibardine, unfurled Prince Charlie's standard in Glenfinnan in 1745. John, 4th Duke, raised the Atholl Highlanders. The 8th Duke originated the Scottish National Memorial in Edinburgh Castle. The seat of the Duke of Atholl is Blair Castle, Perthshire.

Chief : Duke of Atholl.
Patronymic : Am Moireach Mor.
Clan Seats : Blair Castle, Blair Atholl, Perthshire ; Tullibardine, Perthshire ; Duffus Castle, by Elgin.
Plant : Butcher's Broom.
Memorials : Tullibardine Old Kirk.
Pipe Music : Duke of Atholl's Salute.

OGILVY

CORTACHY CASTLE

THE recorded history of the Ogilvies dates back to the days of William the Lion, when mention is made of a certain Gillebride, second son of Gillechrist, Earl of Angus, who assumed the name of Ogilvy from his estate so called. Patrick of Ogilvy, his grandson, was forced to swear fealty to the invader, Edward of England, for his lands in Forfar in 1296. In 1309 Robert I granted a charter to Patrick of Ogilvy of the Barony of Kettins in Forfar. Walter Ogilvy of Wester Pourie was Hereditary Sheriff of Forfar in 1385. His son, Walter Ogilvy was also High Sheriff of Forfar, in 1391, when he lost his life in a conflict with the famous Duncan Stewart. The line of Sir Alexander, eldest son of Sir Walter Ogilvy of Auchterhouse, ended in a daughter, who became Countess of Buchan. The headship of the family then fell to Sir Walter's second son, who was Lord High Treasurer under James I in 1425. He married Isobel Durward, heiress of Lintrathen, by which his posterity were designated until raised to the Peerage, his grandson, Sir James, being made Lord Ogilvy of Airlie in 1491 by James IV. He died in 1504. James, 6th Lord was a loyal subject of Queen Mary. James, 8th Lord, was made Earl of Airlie by Charles I in 1639. The 5th Earl joined Prince Charles at Edinburgh in 1745 with 600 men. The Earl of Airlie, Chief of the clan, has the seats of Cortachy Castle and the " Bonnie Hoose o' Airlie," both in Angus. Other branches of the clan are the Ogilvies of Findlater and Deskford, the Ogilvies of Dunlugas, Ogilvie of Inverquharity, and Ogilvie of Barras.

Chief : Earl of Airlie.
Clan Seats : Airlie Castle, and Cortachy Castle, Angus.
Plant : White Thorn.

RAMSAY

SIMON DE RAMSAY lived in the Lothians in 1140, and William de Ramsay, probably his descendant, swore fealty to King Edward I for his lands of Dalhousie in 1296. He afterwards joined King Robert Bruce. In 1338 his son, Alexander, defended Dunbar against the English, and was afterwards appointed Sheriff of Teviotdale. This offended William Douglas, Knight of Liddesdale, who captured and imprisoned Ramsay, starving him to death in Hermitage Castle. His descendant, Sir Alexander Ramsay of Dalwolsey, had several sons, the eldest of whom, Alexander, carried on the main line of the family. His great-grandson had two sons—George, afterwards Lord Ramsay of Melrose, later Dalhousie, and John, Viscount of Haddington in 1606, and afterwards Earl of Holdernesse. William, 2nd Lord Ramsay, was created Earl of Dalhousie in 1633. George, 8th Earl of Dalhousie, had seven sons. The eldest was George, the 9th Earl, who died in 1838, and was succeeded by his son, James, 10th Earl, who afterwards became Governor-General of India and Marquis of Dalhousie. He died childless, and the estate fell to his nephew, Fox Maule. He also died without issue, and was succeeded by George, 12th Earl, who was son of the Hon. John Ramsay, son of the 8th Earl. Dalhousie Castle, near Edinburgh, is the seat of the Ramsays.

Chief : Earl of Dalhousie.
Clan Seat : Dalhousie Castle, Midlothian.
Plant : Hairbell.

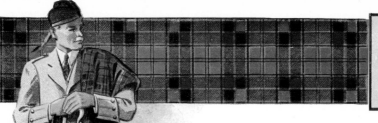

ROBERTSON

THE Chief of the Clan Robertson, known also as the *Clann Donnachaidh*, was *Donnachadh Reamhar*, otherwise known as Duncan de Atholia, who was male descendant of the ancient Celtic Earls of Atholl. The clan, however, count their Chiefs from Duncan, under whom they first appear as a clan in support of Robert the Bruce—Duncan's friend and kinsman. " The Robertsons of Struan," says Skene, " are unquestionably the oldest family in Scotland, being the sole remaining branch of the Royal House which occupied the throne of Scotland during the eleventh and twelfth centuries." From first to last the clan is noted for its loyalty to the Stewarts. On the murder of James I at Perth, it was Robert, the Chief of *Clann Donnachaidh*, who captured his murderers, for which act he had many honours conferred on him by King James I's successor; and to further commemorate this, father and son took the name of Robertson, which the clan has since retained. Their territory it is said, at one time extended from the watershed of Rannoch Moor to the gates of Perth. One of the most famous Chiefs was Alexander Robertson of Struan, known as the " Poet Chief." The Chiefs had castles in Rannoch and at Invervack, near Struan; later, and up to 1860, their principal residence was Dunalastair; other residences were Carie, Dall and Rannoch Barracks. The Chief of the clan is styled Struan-Robertson.

Chief : Robertson of Struan.
Patronymic : Struan-Robertson.
Clan Seats : Dunalastair, Perthshire ; Rannoch Barracks, Perthshire.
Tryst : Dunalastair, Perthshire.
Slogan : Garg'n uair dhuisgear.
Plant : Bracken.
Pipe Music : The Robertsons' Gathering.

103

Constant and true

ROSE

THE predecessors of the Roses of Kilravock settled in Nairnshire during the reign of King David I, the documentary history of the race commencing in the reign of Alexander II, at which time they held the lands of Geddes in Inverness. The Kilravock family have enjoyed their property through a descent of 27 generations. Hugh, the son and successor of Hugh Rose of Geddes, married Mary, daughter of Sir Andrew de Bosco of Redcastle, and thus obtained Kilravock, which was erected into a Barony in 1474. His son, William, had two sons, Andrew, the second, ancestor of the Roses of Auchlossan in Mar, and Hugh, his successor, whose son married Janet, daughter of Sir Robert Chisholm, Constable of Urquhart Castle, by whom he received a large accession to his lands. He left a son, Hugh, who was succeeded by his son, John, who married Isabella Cheyne of Esslemont. Hugh, son of this marriage, built the old tower of Kilravock in 1460. The castle is still inhabited. The Chiefs of the clan, as is usual in the Highlands, have always been styled " The Baron of Kilravock."

Chief : Rose of Kilravock (*Baron of Kilravock*).
Patronymic : The Baron of Kilravock.
Clan Seat : Kilravock Castle, Gollanfield, Nairnshire.
Plant : Wild Rosemary.
Memorials : Barevan, Strathnairn.

ROSS

THE Clan Ross was designated by the Highlanders *Clann Aindreas*, and in the ancient genealogical history they are called *Clann Anrias*. It begins with Paul MacTire, to whom William, Earl of Ross, Lord of Skye, granted a charter for the lands of Gairloch in 1366. In Robertson's *Index* there is mention of a Ferquhard Ross, supposed to be the son of Gille Anrias, from whom the clan took its name. He founded the Abbey of Fearn, in Ross-shire, in the reign of Alexander II. This line ended with Euphemia, Countess of Ross, who resigned the Earldom to an uncle. The Rosses of Balnagowan, a very ancient line, sprang from William, Earl of Ross, a friend of Robert I. His son, Hugh, was killed at Halidon Hill in 1333. From Hugh Ross, second son of Hugh, Earl of Ross, the Balnagowan estates passed on from father to son to David, the last Laird of Balnagowan, who died without issue, when the estate and chiefship passed under entail along with the arms to Brigadier Charles Ross, son of George, 10th Lord Ross of Hawkhead. This line expired and the chief arms were confirmed by Lyon Court to Miss Ross of Pitcalnie. The Rosses of Shandwick, Rosses of Invercharron, and Rosses of Pitcalnie are all branches from the Balnagowan family. Ross of Pitcalnie represent the ancient line of Balnagowan.

Chief : Ross of that Ilk.
Patronymic : Mac Gillanreas.
Clan Seats : Balnagowan Castle, Ross-shire ; Delny, Ross-shire ; Pitcalnie, by Tain.
Tryst : St. Duithacs, Tain, Ross-shire.
Plant : Juniper.
Memorials : Fearn Abbey, Edderton.
Pipe Music : The Earl of Ross's March.

SCOTT

THE Scott history begins in 1130, when there lived one Uchtredus filius Scoti, father of Richard, who is said to have had two sons—Richard, ancestor of the Scotts of Buccleuch, and Sir Michael, ancestor of the Scotts of Balweary. From Richard descended Sir David Scott of Branxholm and Alexander of Howpaisley. From Sir David descended Sir Walter, created Lord Scott of Buccleuch in 1600. His descendant Francis, 2nd Earl of Buccleuch, left a daughter Anne, Countess of Buccleuch, married to James, Duke of Monmouth, son of King Charles II. They were created Duke and Duchess of Buccleuch ; and though he was beheaded, *her* Dukedom has been handed down in regular course from father to son. Alexander's (of Howpaisley) descendant in the eighth degree was Francis of Thirlestane, who was created a Baronet in 1666. His son and successor, Sir William, assumed the name of Napier on his marriage with Elizabeth, Mistress of Napier. Walter Scott of Synton, great-grandson of Richard above-mentioned, was ancestor of Walter of Harden, whose great-grandson was ancestor of the Scotts of Gala. Sir William's (fifth of Harden) youngest son was great-grandfather of Sir Walter Scott, author of *Waverley*, etc. The Balweary Scotts are descended from Sir Michael, grandson of Uchtredus filius Scoti. Branxholm Castle is the ducal seat of the Chiefs of the Clan Scott.

Chief : Scott of Buccleuch.
Patronymic : Duke and Earl of Buccleuch.
Clan Seat : Branxholm Castle, by Hawick.
Tryst : Bellendaine.
Slogan : Bellendaine.
Plant : Blaeberry.
Memorials : Buccleuch Old Kirkyard.

SINCLAIR

WILLIAM, son of the Comte de Sancto Claro in Normandy, and a cousin of Yoland de Bren, Queen to Alexander III, was the progenitor of the Sinclair Clan. Their original seat was Roslin Castle; and they inherited the Norse Earldom of Orkney. William Sinclair, 3rd Earl of Orkney, who founded the collegiate Church of Roslin in 1441 (the youngest " prentice " being by masonic rites slaughtered under " The Prince's Pillar "), was Lord High Treasurer of Scotland in 1445, and Ambassador to England. In 1456 he was made Earl of Caithness. He married Lady Margaret, daughter of Archibald, Earl of Douglas, Duke of Touraine. He died before 1480, and was succeeded by his son, William, 2nd Earl of Caithness, who was slain at Flodden. John, 3rd Earl, was killed during an insurrection in Orkney. His son, George, 4th Earl, supported Mary Queen of Scots, and Bothwell. He died, 1583, leaving two sons—John, Master of Caithness, and George, ancestor of Sinclair of Mey. He was succeeded by his son, George, 5th Earl. George, 6th Earl, had no children, and died in debt. George, 7th Earl, died childless, and his honours fell to John Sinclair of Murkle. In 1789 the Earldom passed to Sir James Sinclair, 7th Baronet of Mey, as 12th Earl; and on the death of George, 15th Earl, to the Sinclairs of Durran, of whom James Augustus became 16th Earl of Caithness and Chief of Clan in 1889.

Chief : Earl of Caithness.
Patronymic : Morair Ghallaobh.
Clan Seats : Girnigoe Castle, Wick, and Brawl Castle, Caithness ; Roslin Castle, Midlothian ; Ravensheugh Castle, Dysart, Fife.
Slogan : Roslin, Roslin.
Plant : Furze (Whin).
Memorials : Roslin Chapel.
Pipe Music : The Sinclairs' March.

SKENE

THIS family took their name from the lands of Skene, in the Earldom of Mar, which they possessed from the thirteenth century till 1827, when, by the death of the last Skene of that Ilk, the estates passed to his nephew, the Earl of Fife. In 1318, King Robert I by charter to Robert Skene of that Ilk made the lands and loch of Skene a Barony. In 1513, Alexander Skene of that Ilk fell at Flodden. A branch of the old family of Skene, designed as of Curriehill, were celebrated lawyers. Sir John Skene of Curriehill was a prominent advocate in the reign of James VI. In 1594 he was appointed Lord Clerk Register, and issued a collection of the Scots Acts of Parliament. His son, Sir James Skene, succeeded the Earl of Melrose as President of the Court of Session in 1626. Alexander Skene of that Ilk is mentioned in 1633 in the *Book of the Annual-Rentaris for Aberdeenshire*, along with others of the same name. In 1641 Andrew Skene of Auchtertool was dubbed Knight at Holyrood by Charles I. William Forbes Skene, Historiographer Royal, will always hold a foremost place among notable Scotsmen of the nineteenth century. He was author of several works of Scotland's history. Skene of Hallyards and Pitlour is the only branch of the family which retains its lands in Scotland.

Chief : Skene of Skene.

Clan Seats : Skene House, Aberdeenshire ; Hallyards Castle, Fife.

THE ROYAL TARTAN

IN old collections this sett is styled " The Royal " Tartan. As such it has always been that worn by the Pipers of Her Majesty's Regiments of Foot, and was— quite correctly—described some years ago by the late King George V as " my personal tartan." In " arisaid sett "—upon a white background—it was also the tartan of our Scottish Queens. Our sovereigns went yearly to the Highlands for the " Autumn Hunting," when, as was the old manner of the chase in Scotland, the whole clan joined in rounding up the deer. Our Royal House is the oldest in Europe ; and the great portrait gallery at Holyrood symbolises the 106 sovereigns who " transmitted us this realm unconquered." On the death of Henry Benedict, last of the Royal House of Stewart, he bequeathed the old Coronation Ring to George III. According to Tanistry, *i.e.* nomination by the Chief, the Celtic Sovereignty was thus passed down into our present Royal Family, who through Princess Elizabeth, daughter of James VI, inherit the blood of Scotland's ancient sovereign dynasty. The sketch illustrates a piper of the Royal Highlanders (Black Watch).

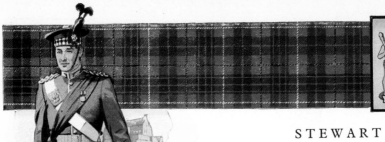

STEWART

THE ancestor of the race was a Breton noble, Alan, a cadet of the ancient Counts of Dol and Dinan. Walter Fitz-Alan received from David I the office of High Steward of Scotland, and was progenitor of the House of Stewart. Alexander, the fourth Steward, left two sons—James, his successor, and Sir John of Bonkyl. From James descended the Royal Stewarts, from Sir John the Bonkyl branch. Walter, the sixth Steward, married Princess Marjory Bruce. Their son reigned as Robert II. From his accession until the death in 1808 of Prince Charlie's brother, the Cardinal of York, the Chiefs of Clan Stewart were heads of the Royal House of Stewart (Stuart). On the Cardinal's death the nearest lawful heir bearing the name was concluded to be George, 8th Earl of Galloway, whose successors in the peerage have been received as the subsequent Chiefs of the clan. The Stewarts of Garlies, created Earls of Galloway 1623, descend from Sir John Stewart of Bonkyl. From Sir James, fourth son of Sir John of Bonkyl, sprang the Stewart Lords of Lorne, and the Stewart Earls of Atholl, Buchan and Traquair. The Highland Stewarts of Appin derive from Dougal, a son of Sir John of Lorne, murdered 1463. Duncan Stewart, 2nd of Appin, was Chamberlain of the Isles to James IV. Subsequent Chiefs of the house of Appin and Ardshiel fought for Charles I under Montrose, and for the Chevalier in the Risings of 1715 and 1745. Though the lands are lost, they still bear the title, Stewart of Appin and Ardshiel. The sketch shows an officer of the Royal Scots regiment in full dress, wearing Hunting Stewart tartan.

Chief : Stewart of Appin.
Patronymic : MacIain-Stiubhart-na-h'Apunn.
Clan Seat : Castle-Stalcaire, by Appin, Argyll.
Tryst : The Cormorant's Rock.
Slogan : Creag-an-Sgairbh.
Plant : Oak.

SUTHERLAND

THE founder of the line of Sutherland, was Hugh, son or grandson of Freskin de Moravia, who, probably by marriage, obtained the clan territory about the time of William the Lion. Hugh's son, William, was created Earl of Sutherland about 1237, and died 1248. William, 2nd Earl, won a great victory over the Danes at Ree-cross. William, 3rd Earl, fought at Bannockburn, and his brother Kenneth, 4th Earl, fell at Halidon Hill. Robert, 6th Earl, fought at Otterburn. Nicholas, 7th Earl, had a feud with the Mackays, which was carried on by his son, Robert. John, 12th Earl, fought at Corrichie in 1562. William, 16th Earl, Chief of the clan in 1745, supported George II. His son William, 17th Earl, left a daughter Elizabeth (his only child), whose right to the earldom was established in 1771. She married George Granville, Marquis of Stafford, and was ancestress of the Dukes of Sutherland. Dunrobin Castle is the seat of the *Morair Chat*, Chief of the clan.

Chief : Sutherland of that Ilk, Earl of Sutherland.
Patronymic : Morair Chat.
Clan Seat : Dunrobin Castle, Sutherland.
Tryst : The Brig o' Dunrobin.
Slogan : Ceann na Drochaide Bige.
Plant : Butcher's Broom.
Memorials : Dornoch Cathedral.
Pipe Music : The Earl of Sutherland's March.

URQUHART

THIS clan takes its name from the district so-called in Ross-shire. The Urquharts of Cromarty at one time possessed nearly all the old county of Cromarty. Thomas Urquhart was Bishop of Ross in 1449, and in 1585 Alexander Urquhart was last Dean of Ross. History makes frequent reference to Sir Thomas Urquhart of Cromarty and his family. John Urquhart of Craigfintry, who built Craigston Castle about 1604, is recorded in the Roll of Landlords as guardian to his grand-nephew, afterwards Sir Thomas Urquhart of Cromarty, father of the famous knight of the same name. In the army of Gustavus Adolphus of 1626 we find Colonel Urquhart " a valiant soldier, expert commander, and learned scholar." Sir Thomas Urquhart of Cromarty attempted the destruction of Inverness Castle in 1649. He is given a place as an author and poet of some repute in the seventeenth century. He forfeited his estate during Cromwell's rule on account of financial difficulties. In 1678 the Laird of Cromarty and Alexander Urquhart of Newhall were Commissioners in Parliament. The heir-male, Urquhart of Braelangwell, in 1957 established his right to the chiefship before Lyon Court, and was officially recognised in the style Urquhart of that Ilk. He has been reponed in Castle-Craig, the Urquhart ancestral fortress, at Urquhart-on-the-firth-of-Cromarty.

Chief : Urquhart of that Ilk.
Clan Seat : Castle-Craig of Urquhart, Black Isle, Ross-shire.
Plant : Wallflower.
Memorials : Cullicudden Old Kirkyard.